ON

A BRILLIANT WAY
TO LIVE & WORK

DR. LEWIS LOSONCY AND COLIN WALSH

PRESS LLC

SANFORD • FLORIDA

Published by DC Press
2445 River Tree Circle
Sanford, FL 32771
www.dcpressbooks.com / www.focusonethics.com

For general information on DC Press publications and services, including this title, please contact our offices at 407-688-1156 or info@dcpressbooks.com.

ISBN: 978-1-932021-65-3
Library of Congress Control Number: In Process

Cover Design: Greg Schultz
Composition & Internal Design: Debra Deysher
Illustrations by Austin "Smoke" Bechtold

First DC Press Printing 2010
10 9 8 7 6 5 4 3 2 1

Printed in the United States of America

Dedication

With Love To

Diane Losoncy and Gabi Losoncy,
Melissa, Tyler, Ryan, and Sean Baker

– Lewis Losoncy

With Love To

Caroline, Jonah and Sienna Walsh
And to the entire Matrix Family

– Colin Walsh

ON

"As far as we can discern, the sole purpose of human existence is to kindle a light in the darkness of mere being."

– Carl Jung

Three Men at Work

Three men were out in the field tilling the soil.

A person passing by stopped and asked the first man, "What are you doing?"

He responded, "I'm tilling the soil."

The curious stranger turned to the second man, asking him the same question. Without hesitation, he answered, "What am I doing? I'm earning a living."

When he finally got the third man's attention, and asked what he was doing, the tiller paused, smiled, and responded, "I'm feeding our community!"

While all three worked the same amount of time, in the same field, doing the same amount of work, the first person's days seemed longer than the second man's days. The third man so loved his work that he wasn't aware of the time.

Near the end of their lives, the first man thought his whole lifetime work was meaningless. The second man said he was able to feed his family through his work. But, the third man felt very peaceful because he lived an inspired life by making the world a better place doing his lifework.

They were all doing the same work.

Being ON is the electrifying result of connecting our passion to our purpose. Its power allows us to perform at our most brilliant and always lights a clear path of action toward any goal.

– Colin Walsh

When we are turned ON, our spirits are empowered with a great purpose. That's real power! Our spirits are our unlimited collective resources that transcend, and add strength to, our limited physical bodies, and fragile psychological egos to reach our dreams.

– Lewis Losoncy

Most people have moments when they are free of ego...while they are performing their work. They may, or may not know it, but their work has become their spiritual practice...I have met teachers, artists, doctors, scientists, social workers, waiters, hairdressers, business owners and salespeople who perform their work admirably without any self-seeking, fully responding to whatever the moment requires of them. They are one with what they do, one with the Now, one with the people or task that they serve...Anyone who is one with whatever he or she does is building the new earth.

– Eckhart Tolle,
The New Earth

WE CAN GIVE OURSELVES A <u>RAISE</u>!

By Finding a <u>Higher Purpose</u> for Our Work

> *A paycheck is poor medication for unhappiness.*
>
> *— Colin Walsh*

Think about it. **Why** do we get up and go to work each day?

We might quickly respond, "To make money, of course!" — *the Bread.*

But is that all there is? Are we living by bread alone? Is that it?

Well, after reflecting a bit, we might add that we go to work to make, market, package, sell or deliver something, or maybe to teach or manage others.

Those are great answers to "**What** do we do?" But the question is, "**Why** do we do what we do?"

Perhaps our answer goes back to earning the "bread," and stops there.

Certainly "bread" is important, but again, is that all there is?

While we can get by and survive in life eating bread alone, wouldn't it be more enriching to get more than our bimonthly dough?

Doesn't a fulfilling meal include much more than just "getting filled up" with bread? Could the possibilities of an appealing appetizer, an exciting entrée and tasty dessert turn our ordinary meal into an inspirational culinary experience?

Sharing the delightful setting with people we respect and enjoy in a flickering candle light setting might warm up the evening even more. Why not add some of our favorite background music to round out the perfect dining experience? But, if we have to, maybe we could *survive* on the bread alone.

We believe that the same is true in the workplace. There can be more to our experiences that just working for *the bread* alone. So much of our energies are spent there. How much would it benefit us to take a different view of our work, and find more purpose and, maybe even more satisfaction? At the very least, we could make our days go faster! And the great news is that creating more meaningful days at work are up to only one person. You or Me!

What if we found more meaning in our work, to turn us, our teammates, and our workspaces to *ON*, rather than to be switched *OFF*? When our work setting is turned ON, it can offer us so much more than just bread. Like the inspiring table setting for dinner, the workspace can go beyond giving us just the basics. While the bread satisfies our money needs, the appetizer and entrée satiate our growth needs, the dessert delights our psychological needs, our companions fulfill our social needs, and the flickering candlelight and soft music can soothe our inspirational needs.

Why would we still want just the bread at home or at work? Wouldn't it be better, for us, to experience so much more by turning our work life into our lifework? We can give ourselves a *raise*, simply by going in to work lifted up by a higher purpose to make a small portion of our world better.

- Could achieving our dreams together mean more than we met our monthly or quarterly financial goals and now can breath a sigh of relief for another day? Or can reaching our dreams together buy us collective feelings of pride, camaraderie and closeness?

- Are our contributions in the workplace reduced to what we do with our heads and hands? Or can our own attitude and love of the work process or the products we create, build, market, sell and service enhance our personal experiences in the working atmosphere?

- Can our view of our customers, clients, cases or market inspire us to realize our impact on the world?

- Is our customer reduced to being, "a number, an invoice, someone or something out there?" Or can we feel our customer's heartbeat? Do we experience our customer as another breathing, alive person, whose quality of life we are going to enrich, advance or protect? And whose very product or service needs we find personal satisfaction in fulfilling?

- Must the workplace inevitably be heartless? Or can we transform our work atmosphere with the higher purpose of building a better world?

- Can feeling passionate about our work affect our performance? Is it possible that our passion wrings out our creative juices and energies to overcome our challenges together to reach our collective dreams?

- Can our courage play any role in our company success? Doesn't it take courage to create better ways for our team to go forward?

The underlying point of these thoughts is that there is something higher in us that is hungry too. And the money — *the bread*, just doesn't do it, because that hunger is coming from a place that transcends our physical bodies. We know that place very well. We have spent the highest and lowest moments of our lives living in this space. That *place* is where our spirits come to life when we decide to turn them ON. Or that same place can be where our spirits stay dark as we live out our lives robotically shut OFF. In Chapter 2 we will discover the location of our spirits, but where is the proof that they even exist?

How often do we hear references to our spirits in everyday conversations? In those moments, what common meanings do both parties hold, understand, can relate to, and associate with when hearing the word, *spirit*? Well, we experience the root word "spirit" in many moving concepts from "aspired," to "inspired," "spirited," or even "dispirited." We talk about one team that has lost its spirit, and describe another as being "high-spirited." We are lifted by an inspiring concert, or aroused by a spirited conversation. Experiencing ordinary people doing extraordinary things can encourage us to aspire to achieving greater things in our own lives. We use the word inspiration frequently, and we recall those moments when our spirits were lifted, proving our spirits exist, and are an important, yet neglected, part of us.

But how can we connect inspiration with times we are at work? What is that all about? Is it possible? If so, wouldn't it be awesome to be able to take the same old work, and to find inspiration and higher purpose in it?

. . . .

Inspiration turns us ON, wherever we are. When entering a dark room, we say, "Turn ON the light!" A simple flick of the switch turns darkness into light. We see more clearly, become more aware, walk more securely, and move more directly to our destination. When the light is ON. Think of how much slower and more treacherous the same path would be if the light was OFF. We can do the same thing in the same old workplace. We can turn the lights ON.

In life, and in our own workspaces, we subconsciously put ourselves into either an ON or an OFF mode. The quality and meaning of our day, and our lifetime, hinge on that flickering decision. Observe any work, from two different parents, one switched ON, the caring nurturer who finds fulfillment soothing the tearful little one, and the other, turned OFF and angry at the same annoying "little brat." Listen to two car salesmen as they make generalizing statements about customers, one seeing them as opportunities, the other as pains. In the same showroom! You immediately sense who is ON and who is OFF.

OFF: *"We're supposed to push desserts again."*
ON: *"I can't wait to tell everyone about our delicious key lime pie!"*

The fact that one coal miner swears he hates every minute of his time there, and his partner feels at home in the underground cavern, reveals more about each man than it does the nature of their work. In fact, perhaps one of the most rewarding choices of our lives is the decision to take whatever circumstances we are facing, and turn ON the bright side. Since we are there anyway, why not look up?

A *turned ON culture* is composed of can-do, find-a-way people who choose to make the most of their time together. They transform their old workspaces into world changing settings. They view each other as teammates, as great sports teams do, and they focus on the achievements of the day, rather than waiting until the weekend at home to find fulfillment. They turn ON, rather than OFF, and create a bright workspace for each other. We say bright because isn't that the smart thing to do?

Written from the positive energies of Lewis Losoncy and Colin Walsh, **ON** is designed to be as practical, as it is inspirational, for you, in whatever work space you are living. Lewis Losoncy is a motivational psychologist, and author of two dozen books on encouragement, motivation and leadership. "Dr. Lew" reveals to you how these inspiring ideas can bring a new life, and a passionate purpose to your workplace.

Colin Walsh is the energetic and dynamic leader of Matrix USA, one of the largest companies in the professional salon industry and a division of L'Oreal. The bright-eyed visionary elevates us to discover our higher purpose, to realize our ultimate "why" we go to work each day. Colin offers the empowering insight that our inspired presence in the workspace can be the source of great things in the world. By turning others and ourselves to ON, we can transform the culture of our work communities into more positive places. And we can bring more than just bread, and receive more than just the dough. We can lift the spirits of others with whom we work each day to realize we are making a difference in the world!

When ON. we give ourselves an immediate raise. We have found the higher purpose to making our part of the world a little bit better for others and ourselves.

ON

AN INSPIRING NEW WAY TO WORK

ON moments are those special uplifting times when one person inspires another to realize she or he matters. These simple, every day inspiring incidents occur in many ways. They range from hearing, "Our floors are spotless because of you," to "We are going to use your great ideas on saving shipping costs;" or "we missed you, the place wasn't the same here without you;" to "You touched over 10,000 people by getting those flyers out."

Other ON moments might include, "Wow, sounds like you and Jonah had a great time discovering the wonders of the sea at the Science Museum today" to "You were on fire at our sales meeting yesterday." Maybe even, "That was an amazing, life-saving landing you made on the Hudson River!"

These ON moments raise our spirits, making the workspaces more inspiring, and purposeful. You could say that when we are ON, we are changing another person's world. In other words, we are changing the world! We are taking the same old circumstances, and adding new life to ourselves, and others.

This book offers an uplifting view of our times at work. Why not? A huge portion of our energies are spent there. What if we started finding ways to find new meaning in our work, and to treasure those with whom we are making the world a little better place? **How much would an inspired view of our work be worth to us personally?**

Many would argue that the workspace setting is inevitably a bottom-lined, efficiency-obsessed environment, with a linear purpose, propelled by self-defensive egos, dog-eat-dog, head butting, backbiting and credit hogging. Or worse yet, it might be defined as a place where no one ever cares to notice our everyday performance. How can we make the same old workspace an inspiring place, where people want to grow together to create a better world?

We are advocating a more enriching, holistic view of people at work. A vantage point that goes beyond the way we always thought about work before. A higher perspective that puts people at the heart of the enterprise of changing the world together, while experiencing a more personally fulfilling work life.

When ON, we are enlightened to spot many other light switches, not only for ourselves, but for others in our workspaces. There are many ways to lighten up our workplace, and we are only limited to our creative minds and our caring hearts. Consider some points of inspiration:

LOCATING THE "ON" SWITCHES

ON opportunities are the areas where we can help another community member to realize that his or her work, and life, really counts.

1. Inspirational Switches

Connecting your own and others' work to its impact on the world:

"I'll bet your students will remember today's class on bees forever. You opened my eyes. I've never seen bees as being so important before, such as pollinating flowers."

2. Professional Growth Switches

Connecting with how you and your teammates are growing through your work:

"I never, ever thought you guys could get all of those holiday shipments out today. All of you have streamlined and improved our delivery process. Thanks guys, there will be a lot of excited children in three days because of you."

3. Social Switches

Connecting work with your positive contributions to the team:

"Thanks, Naika, for getting every fine detail covered for the meeting. You always, always come through for us!"

4. Psychological-Emotional Switches

Connecting work with developing confidence, security and pride:

"Daniel, look at the confidence you have gained in your performance. You are now one of the best presenters I have ever seen."

5. Financial Switches (traditional focus)

Connecting work to money:

"Your check is in the mail."

TABLE OF CONTENTS

FRONT MATTER

PART I

BUILD OUR INSPIRATION POWER SOURCE
Connecting our why? to our spirit.

PART II

PLUG IN
Be Aware of Our 5 Power Sockets

"Today is the most important day of our lives. It is the only day we can change now!"

"Our view of our work is our most important resource."

"Let's move from our strengths and potentials"

"What is, is!"

"Our challenges have solutions."

PART III

HIT THE "ON" SWITCH
8 Electric Lights to Turn on Our Workplace

PART IV

RECHARGE
Our Backup Light in Case of Power Failure

PART I

BUILD OUR INSPIRATION POWER SOURCE

Connecting our why? to our spirit.

Our Workspace: Where Our Spirits Meet Our Why?

Our Helping Spirit: Bringing More than Our Hands to Work

Knowing "Why to do!" Precedes Knowing "What to do!"

Knowing from where our motivational energy at work is generated helps us turn it ON and keep it turned ON.

Here in Part I, we will master the exact locations of the *three sources of power* available to us — that can be unleashed at any time.

These are *our workspace, our spirits*, and *our why* — or — *our higher purpose*.

Chapter 1 shows us how we can change the world from our same workspace.

Chapter 2 reveals to us the very location of our own source of inspiration, that is, our spirits. And, in

Chapter 3, we discover how to ignite these spirits by finding or creating our why? — or our higher human purpose at work.

Our task to start the switched ON process is simply to make the connections between our *spirit* and our *why?* in our *workspace*. As a jumper cable works, we will be sparking the ignition to turn our work spirit ON.

CHAPTER I

OUR WORKSPACE:

Where our Spirits Meet Our Why

> *Ask not what your country can do for you.*
> *Ask what you can do for your country.*
>
> *– John F. Kennedy*

Turning ON moments are those simple, everyday meaningful messages in which one person offers another person an inspiring thought or insight.

"I thought that I would be just bundling bars of steel with a bunch of other part-timers at Carpenter Steel. I was happy. I had a job during my college summer vacations. And then on my first morning Mr. Umbenauer gathered us "bundlers" together and explained, 'what you guys will be wrapping today will be part of automobiles that you may eventually see on the road. Thanks guys!'"

"Every day, Mr. U. would tell us not just what we need to get done, but <u>why</u> we were doing it. The day I'll remember most was when the burly enthusiastic boss confided, 'Today most of what you guys will be wrapping up to ship out is a specialty product to be part of the first spacecraft that we will be landing on the moon!'"

"Each day I would tell my girl about my work. When I saw cars driving down the street, I would occasionally joke that the car would not have been possible without me. And on July 20, 1969, when Neil Armstrong took his first steps on the lunar surface and proclaimed, 'One small step for a man, one giant leap for mankind,' my girlfriend hugged and thanked me. What could have been a boring, routine job turned into a rich and eye-opening experience that I remember a half-century later. Because of my inspiring pit boss!"

"If you want to do hair, you can work anywhere. If you want to change peoples' lives by realizing that you are giving them courage, confidence and hope through your skills in styling and coloring, then we would be honored to have you working with our salon family. As a salon artist, you are in one of only five professions that touch people, along with the doctor, dentist, nurse and massage therapist. You will be touching your clients' lives anywhere from six to fifty times a year, more frequently then they see their relatives. And you have the skills and tools to make them beautiful. Can you imagine a more important gift than that? That's what you will be doing here at our salon."

"Having been a hairdresser for years, I moved from salon to salon based on the amount of commission I would get. But after listening to Carmen speak, I found a new type of reward. A different kind of paycheck Carmen had. I was inspired for the first time in my life to touch peoples' lives in a more meaningful way!"

These two inspiring moments: one for the college student in his summer job of bundling bars of steel, and the other involving the hairdresser whose eyes were opened to the beauty of her work, could have occurred anywhere, on any job, career or profession in any workplace environment. The creative, inspiring teammate is offering a richer vision of another's work.

These uplifting times may occur in the corporate office, the store, the shop, the mill, the car, at the kitchen table, in the classroom, locker room, church, or most importantly in the backyard — giving a young one a little push in the work space behind the wobbly swing.

The person with a hand on the light switch is not limited to a role or position, but rather is anyone determined to become an inspiration to others. Everyone is a potential leader, when it comes to finding the way to a more positive environment. The fact is: the light goes ON no matter who flicks the switch.

Far too many people view what "they do for a living" as: "going to work, to make money, to pay bills." Their times at work are filled with boredom, anxiety, and perhaps a sense of meaninglessness and insignificance. Some may wonder, "Why am I here?" as they sort through their moment-to-moment workplace experiences. They do, however, have at least one short-term goal — which they might refer to as, "Three o'clock!" or "Five o'clock!" Their work is connected to nothing more than a paycheck, and their rewards are limited to a single day every two weeks.

It can all be different.

Yes, our experiences in the workplace can be enriched, even with the same people, in the same spaces. Something more meaningful happens when a person makes a commitment to inspire another person's view of his or her work, life, and lifework.

In *Spirited Leading and Learning*, Peter Vaill asks his readers to recall the greatest and most memorable moments they have experienced in their work. A sample of the responses to the questions included (1) "Feeling that my work was valuable," (2) "The teamwork was so strong it bordered on love," (3) "Extraordinary leadership who kept us positive and enthusiastic," and (4) "Being transformed by the task, like entering another plane of existence."

Rarely did Dr. Vaill hear about facts or numbers or effects of organizational charts as being the source of personal meaning. Rather, these lifting moments came from a higher place inside the person, usually expressed in feelings, which are reflections of the spirit. People in their treasured workspaces, like people in all settings, are, as philosopher Pierre Teilhard de Chardon would describe, "spiritual beings in physical bodies."

An ON culture has a desire to build spirited people who connect their work to the larger world, inspire a feeling of pride in achievement, encourage others to experience fulfillment in being together, and realize the change their presence and their contributions produce in society.

Tom Peters and Robert Waterman, authors of the best seller, *In Search of Excellence*, made a curiously interesting observation. After observing their choices for "outstanding companies," they concluded that the cultures with the best organizations valued training — that was "almost mystical."

Corporate culture? "Almost mystical?" What is going on here?

We believe that this mystical climate is evoked in an atmosphere of inspiration. Obviously, the turned ON community's vantage point transcends the engineer Frederick Taylor's view that reduced the human at work to a machine. The model designed by psychologist Abraham Maslow, exposing the human at work's physical, social, emotional, self-esteem, self-actualization needs, touched on the spiritual needs of people in the workplace. Maslow understood this wonderful "mystical" aspect of our lives, as being part of our human nature — even more significant than our hands and feet.

We believe that when something "mystical" is happening anywhere, our spirits are energized to reach further, grabbing more creative meaning from our higher human possibilities. If so, then "mystical" simply means we are energized to go beyond our previous perceptions of our limits. You might say we are finding a higher place of potential inside us. When we look up and see that new place, we are finding our spirit. When our spirits are aroused, our engines are ignited to transport us way beyond our tired physical bodies, our difficult economic times, even the impossible challenges we face together. Creating an atmosphere for the growth of our spirit is the solid foundation from where the well-lit workspace is built to grow.

Something is very clear. In the midst of the huge challenges in today's world, there must be a better way. We are given more to do. Bodies and minds, fatigued treading the rising water of challenges, call desperately for more outside resources. Exhausted, we often feel we are in the dark.

And then a light switch turns ON.

Enter the person who brings the flashlight into the dark workspace. The first thing we notice, after being temporary blinded by the rare promising light, is the person holding the hope. The bright-eyed dreamer offers us a compelling dream, and a passionate purpose. The workspaces slowly warm up, everyone of us sensing we are being handed the link that was missing between our work, and our significance! The shared inspiring vision becomes our mortar, cementing a bunch of individuals into a compassionate family, full of purpose. Each of us are co-authors of this new creation to contribute at higher, more meaningful levels. Our spirits widen, like the flowers opening up in early spring. And when our spirits are aroused, thoughts and dreams are envisioned buoyed up by hope, optimism, courage, love and inspiration. Meaning, purpose and significance are experienced by our community in the hallways again — like the day the idea of the company was originally conceived!

All of this is happening in the very, very special safe, sacred haven that we once referred to as the shop, office, cubicle, or even the dungeon, the mill, or even the prison cell. The light is not only energizing, but soon becomes infectious. Each community member is renewed with the realization that we can contribute to building a better team. The tipping point is reached. Change is in the air. Right there, at work, of all places.

Come join us in our journey. Bring your flashlight to your work site. That's the bright thing to do, isn't it?

CHAPTER 2

OUR HELPING SPIRIT:

Bringing More than Our Hands to Work

> *Good business leaders create a vision,*
> *articulate the vision, passionately own the vision,*
> *and relentlessly drive it to completion.*
>
> *— Jack Welch*

When you get a phone call at 5 PM on New Year's Eve, you expect that it's a close relative or special friend on the other end of the line. But at our company, it was different. It was our President. His voice was moved with joy.

"Guess what, I'm with creative, and we just finished the buttons and shirts for our introduction to our theme, 'Find a Way!' They will be ready for our big meeting in Orlando next week. We are all sharing a glass of champagne together to celebrate before we go home. Every one in creative wanted you to know, because you were wondering if it was possible on such short notice. We were determined not to leave until we 'Found a Way!'"

New Year's Eve! Anyone in the company would have been there if they could, just to be a part of the moment. We all knew we were working for an inspiring company. Our work was very important to us and we made a difference in each other's lives. Yes, the skills we learned at the conference (the "hands") were important, but mainly our spirits (the "spirits") were on fire to find a way to change the world together.

. . . .

Almost every company celebrates one annual meeting — extolling the theme that, "People make the difference!" How do people make the difference? What is it that highlights us as the elixir to our company's or family's vigor and success? To be sure, our "hands," or what we do through our abilities, our creative minds, and our skill sets are all a part of the gifts we bring through the work door each day. But is that all there is?

Or — are there more gifts that we offer each day to brighten our work community?

Perhaps the most valuable resources we bring to the motivational alter of our community's success are overlooked. These rich treasures are only occasionally discussed, because, and unlike what we achieve through our "hands," they can't be measured, weighed, or even be seen with the sharpest microscope ever developed. And while these assets are located nowhere, they can be felt everywhere.

And curiously, while we cannot see them, like the wind that makes our airplane bounce and fly, we can experience proof of them. We can't measure them, but we can be moved by their powerful impact. We hear them in those special, empowering moments when something inside inspires us to, "go onward anyway!" The finest, most rewarding moments of our lives are found when we are re-discovering and re-employing these treasures.

These treasures are our spirits! Switching someone ON involves elevating another person's spirits. But how do we do that? Where are their spirits located if we are going to lift them?

Let's understand what we mean by spirit first, and then in the balance of the book we will discuss the ON process.

UNDERSTANDING OUR SPIRIT

Try this little experiment: Imagine you are moving your body twenty steps in any direction. Seriously. Count the twenty steps in your imagination before you read on.

What was your experience like? Perhaps your reaction is, "no big deal," or maybe you were even a little annoyed that we asked you to do something as absurd as that.

Now, before you imagine taking those same twenty steps again, picture the finish line and imagine what it would take to win an Olympic Gold Medal for your country — it consists of those same twenty steps away.

Locate the point you are moving to in your mind, and go! And — We aren't even asking you to play any *Rocky* music.

How did your steps feel this time? Were you moving faster? Did your heart beat quicker? In what ways were you different in the second situation? You were the same You in both instances. It was the same distance in both experiences.

Perhaps in the first try, only your legs or hands were engaged. And, in that second, some higher purpose inside you moved your whole body. This is your spirit. In other words, you were inspired. You were ON! Your spirit was engaged to move you arms and legs with more meaning and purpose.

Another way of understanding the power of our spirit is to consider our own human nature, by focusing on two vital components, (1) our physical self and (2) our spirit. It is our spirit that is the mover and shaker of our physical self, or our "hands."

Perhaps a way of thinking about the relationship between our physical self and our inspirational self is to consider an automobile. When looking at a car, we initially observe the physical appearance, the color, model and style. In fact, we often buy the car based solely on that material, observable factor. The physical car is an important part of the car. But there is much more needed to give that car its life, and fulfill its higher purpose of moving the world. Under the hood exists the motor. This engine determines whether the car "works" or not.

Many people take excellent care of the physical outside of the car, and, because it is "further away," or not as accessible, or perhaps, less understood, pay less attention to the deeper part under the hood. Yet, the car doesn't "work" unless the engine is functioning. It is this — the motor — that moves the car. There are more important factors we need to consider when taking care of our car than to just wash the outside. It is crucial for us to spend time caring for the engine. The engine is the spirit of the car. And it is our spirit, our motor that moves our mind, our heart, and our physical bodies.

There's no question why some things don't work.

We have more than a physical existence, like the outside of the car. Our physical selves crave life's basic "things" like food and shelter, necessitating the needs for financial fulfillment to acquire these essentials. In this, our physical needs are a reflection of our animal nature.

In addition to our animal nature, we also have a human nature, our engine, under (or over) our physical selves. And our human nature transcends our physical needs, finding us endowed with emotional, mental, social and spiritual needs.

This is our spirit, our engine, our reason to move us to live our lives more fully, even beyond the limitations of our body, and our ego. We say "more fully" because our spirit speaks with a higher purpose as reflected in a different vocabulary than the one used by our physical selves. In our spirit, we discover feelings and ideas related to transcendent concepts like courage, belief, trust, integrity, attitude, will, hope, optimism, unity and love. We are emotionally and socially engaged to unleash our mental resources to dream, create, discover, rejoice and celebrate together. We seek connections to the natural human power sources bigger than our physical selves, and psychological egos, to turn us on, and to enlighten us of our human contributions and possibilities.

The exact location of our spirit, our engine, is in our imagination. Our spirits are aroused when we are imagining all that we can be, and all that our lives can be. In the workplace, taking the same old job and imagining all that it can be for our teammates, our customers, the world, and our own selves evoke our spirits.

The ON community is lifted by anyone who brings her or his engines, or spirits, into the workplace. And it is this, our helping spirits that moves our helping hands.

CHAPTER 3

KNOWING "WHY TO DO," PRECEDES KNOWING "WHAT TO DO"

We're talking about a sense of purpose. Every Category of One Company that I've ever worked with has created clarity around the 'Why?' of their business, not just the 'What of their business.'

— Joe Calloway, Author
Category of One Companies

He who has a 'Why' to live can bear almost any 'How?'

— Friedrich Nietzsche

Even before the popular song *YMCA* hit the charts at #1, it was common to hear teenagers in our city shout to each other, "Let's go to the Y and play some b-ball." One day, a young fellow asked, "What is the way to the Y? How do you get there?" He captured the essence of this book, that is, finding the way to the *Why?*

Our purpose — the why? — precedes our progress. Purpose is the cause; progress is the effect. Think about it. The existence of the dream of the building preceded the existence of the actual physical building, didn't it? Buildings don't build dreams; Dreams build buildings. The "why?" precedes the "what?" which then decides the "how?" Most workplaces are impoverished of spirit because they have reduced their work to "what" and "how?

"Here is your job description. These are your responsibilities. We expect you to get out about 55 orders a night. The books are listed alphabetically by author's last name, and here are the boxes for shipping. Clarence will take care of the postage. You'll work the night shift from 3-11 AM. Check in by 2:30 AM. You already know what you'll be making and your benefits. Any other questions?"

Sound familiar in a way? When we are left with just "what? and "how?" — we are missing our spirit. We have forgotten the way to the "why?" We have lost our engines. Our "vision" is nowhere in sight. That's why we can't see why we are there at the grindstone!

The foundation to turn us ON is what we call an inspiring "why?" A "why?" becomes inspiring when it moves our spirits or engines? The inspiring "why?" ignites us by re-framing our "reason for being," from simply having a job to having an impact on the world.

When the inspiring "why?" is constantly renewed and celebrated, every one becomes energized to find *better ways*. Better ideas are the process products of a team that is ON fire.

WHY?　　WHAT?　　HOW?

The Inspiring Purpose　　Strategic Vision and Goals　　Strategic Plan and Processes

An Inspiring "Why" Moves People to Find Better Ways

1.　Connecting to the Inspiring "Why?"

Asking "how," creates a to-do list. Asking "why," creates a purpose. Our energies are highest when our purpose is clearly defined. All efforts and resources are directed towards achieving our collective reason for being. While the financial reason for being is profits — *the bread*, the motivation and inspiration to earn the profits are fired up, when our spirits are ignited — driven from a higher purpose. When our human fires are lit up with meaning, our energies and ideas surface enhancing the chances of achieving both our ultimate purpose, and the resultant profits.

We are turning people ON when we are making a direct link between each person's efforts with her or his higher purpose at work!

"Jake, I'd like to welcome you to our shipping department. You are part of our team here. Miles and Philip, welcome Jake. You'll be working closely with Clarence, our expert in postage. Here is Ari who'll be able to help you see why our work is important. We pride ourselves here Jake with the fact that each of these books that you will be packaging or boxing was some author's dream. He or she spent years writing that book in our hands and had a message to communicate to the world. They found a publisher, did all the hard work. And now they turn their dream over to us.

We are their connection, carrying their important words into the lives of people they have never met. You might be packing a book that will help a person overcome depression, or excite a child's imagination. This is where Philip, Miles, Clarence, Ari and now, you come in Jake. This is why we are here. Each time you pick up a book, look at the title, the author's name and look at the address you are sending it to. And just imagine how important what you are doing at that moment is. Tonight we all are here to help you see what to do and how to do it. That won't take long."

The "What" & "How   **The "Why" Thinker**
Thinker

The "why?" is stated as an ultimate purpose or ideal. For example: a pharmaceutical company might live for "Building a healthier world." The reason is idealized in the sense that every person's actions add bricks to the building of the larger dream. In the manufacturer's purpose, contributing to the inspiring "why?" is evidenced when a new product is being developed, and the lab is envisioning it that will help people to live healthier and longer, thus answering the "why?" "Building a healthier world."

Likewise the marketer, salesperson, the educators, members on Line 20, everyone in the stock room and the delivery persons are all connected, by linking on to the common motivational source of the inspiring "why?" This elicits not only their hands in the process, but their spirits. The workplace becomes more sacred because it is the arena, stage, setting, and alter of world-changing activity. This transformed view of one's contribution doesn't ignore the valuable roles of techniques, strategies, skills and bottom-financial line of profits, but rather is multiplicative, providing power to be the motivational push to achieve the bottom dollar line.

The "why?" is the unified purpose of the community. Understanding the inspiring "why?" may transform seeing one's work as the job of just making and selling sandwiches, to envisioning the same physical activities as nourishing peoples' lives through great service, and food.

One woman might think about her teaching job as helping kids learn math. Another faculty member might envision the classroom as the place where she touches chords in young children that will vibrate into eternity. Each day she has the opportunity to build competence and confidence that the students will pass on to future generations! Same work: One with the classroom light OFF; the other with the light turned ON.

While we hope to inspire you to develop your inspiring "why?" or your motivating reason for being, the opportunity is preciously yours. We just encourage you to develop the higher purpose.

. . . .

☀ **TURNING IT ON**

Developing Your Inspiring "Why?"

Take some time to understand your community's reason for being in a way that it evokes your spirit to connect your work to a higher human purpose. The higher purpose is how your products and services make peoples' lives richer, more beautiful, confident, smarter, safer, happier, healthier, enjoyable, exciting, cleaner, more hygienic, more secure, more hopeful or reassuring, wiser, entertained, more consistent, more predictable, or less painful or tense, reduces anxieties, or fears. Consider any product or service your company provides that adds quality or makes the world a better place for people whether it adds pleasure or reduces pain.

. . . .

2. Connecting to Inspiring People, the "Who?"

Some people are connected by geography, like next-door neighbors. Others are linked by the roles they play, such as being educators, or members of a sales force. In the ON workspace, people are bonded by the spirit of the shared "why?" Under the same visionary umbrella, there exists a mutual respect amongst the different departments. Each person is vital, and is wholly involved in the process in his or her area of expertise. Each person is not viewed as just a part of the process. He or she is the respected owner of what he or she does. Remove anyone's specific gifts, and the product is different in some way, shape or form. Community members respect every contribution as necessary and vital to the achievement of the final purpose.

. . . .

☀ **TURNING IT ON**

Connecting Others to the Higher Purpose – The Inspiring Why?

Make a list of your community members. Take a few moments to renew your company's ultimate human purpose or your inspiring "why?" Now look over the names of your community members, one by one. First reflect on each person's major strengths, talents, interests, resources and potential. Then connect the person's assets to the ultimate purpose. Show how each person's contribution fits into the higher purpose of changing and making the world better. Give examples of the logical extension of the person's work on human lives.

1.
2.
3.
4.
5.
6.
7.
8.
9.
10.

. . . .

3.   Connecting to Inspiring Ideas

Inspiring ideas," are the seeds desired to find better ways to reach our higher purpose. Ideas are not simply important. Ideas, or finding better ways, are everything! Think about it. Our company or our family started off as a seed or germ of an idea. Look at how far we have come by generating newer, better ideas. The Golden Gate Bridge in the San Francisco Area, the Holland Tunnel between New Jersey and New York, the craft that landed the first humans on the moon — they all started off as an idea. Diseases are cured by better ideas, and the fulfillment, happiness and success of an individual, family, team, company, nation, or a world depends upon the collective ideas generated. The psychotherapist's goal is to help the patient change ideas about life. The discouraged person has different ideas than the courageous person.

When ON, fresh ideas flow like the winds of Wyoming. Ideas are real things, abstractions capable of transforming thoughts into things, solid as bricks that can be used to build or destroy the human spirit. The cultural mood is to encourage others to "find better ways!" The deep philosophical ideal communicated constantly is that "there is an ultimate idea that perfects our contribution to the inspiring 'why?' And we are constantly striving to find that idea. Each day we get a few ideas closer!

. . . .

💡 TURNING IT ON

Inspiring Better Ideas:
The Inspiring "What?" and "How?"

So far you have renewed your community's higher purpose and identified how each person uses his or her strengths and potential to move the company towards the inspiring why or ultimate power source. Now create the process to inspire people to think of better ways to reach the dream. Make a commitment to offer one better idea a week. Experience an atmosphere of total safety knowing that while all ideas may not be immediately brought into the community, all ideas are valued because each idea provides a trampoline for future ideas. Plus everyone is contributing to building a better culture.

. . . .

After we fully understand "why'" — our purpose, then we move on to do the easier parts. That is working out the details of "what," to do, and "how" to do it, but now doing it for a different reason. Because — it is important.

We are buoyed up with the healthy, inspiring and growthful life view we share, as we approach each day together. *The power source that provides the energy starts when our inspiring why? connects with our spirits.*

. . . .

Our unlimited power source is transmitted to the workplace through five spirit sockets distributed throughout our work arena. One spirit socket is located on each of the four walls with the fifth socket found on the ceiling. Our soon to be switched ON community has all of the motivational power it needs by simply glancing at any of the five spirit sockets, plug in, and feel the burst. Right there at our same old workspaces.

These five spirit sockets unite our turned ON company by maximizing our motivation and minimizing our frustrations. They are the topics of the next part of our journey. Its time to learn how to plug into our energy, which is generated from the connection of our *inspiring why* with *our spirits* in *our workplace*.

PART II

PLUG IT IN

Be Aware of Your 5 Power Sockets

Our Aliveness Socket

Our Attitude Socket

Our Asset Socket

Our Acceptance Socket

Our Answers Socket

We have just connected our why? — purpose — to our spirit to create our power source. This linking — "why to spirit generator" — is wired to transmit its power to five spirit or power receptacles or sockets in our workplace.

As we enter this wired exciting new workroom, the first thing we need to do is to locate the sockets on the walls to plug into, to harness the energy from our spirits. We can use any of these five spirit sockets as needed. For example, we might look to our right and locate our Aliveness Spirit Socket and gain a burst of energy by realizing that we are alive and today is our wide opened opportunity to achieve great things. Or we might plug into the Attitude Spirit Socket on the wall in front of us and the power we have simply by looking our circumstances in a new way. The Asset Spirit Socket, to our left, releases to us reminders of our strengths. The Acceptance Socket, at first hidden at our backs, will offer the powers of serenity, relaxation and humor. Our Answers Spirit Sockets, up there on the ceiling, near the middle, will help us realize our unlimited creative powers to solve challenges.

CHAPTER 4

OUR ALIVENESS SOCKET

Look for this socket on the wall to your right

Today is our most important day:
It is the only day we can change now!

The secret to fulfillment isn't about
getting what you don't have, but instead
being grateful for what you do have!

– Colin Walsh

Picture the spot where you most frequently stand or sit in your workspace. If you drive to work, simply do the same in your car. Finding your spirit sockets are most challenged while on a merry go round or in a boxing ring. Start by imagining there are five sockets in your workspace. You can use any one to gain the power from your purpose-spirit connection generator, but sometimes one receptacle is more accessible than the others.

As you imagine your usual work spot, look to your right at the wall and near the bottom you will observe your Aliveness Socket. Your aliveness socket is available whenever you need it. You will get power by simply plugging into your awareness that you are alive and that wouldn't have to be. And that today is the most important day of your life because it is the only day you can change now.

Practice using your aliveness socket and, as you look to your right, fully realize your aliveness.

When finding our aliveness socket, we experience an immediate surge of energy. The jolt that a joy for living can give us is electrifying. The awareness of being alive, in itself, is not only inspiring, but is miraculous. This appreciation for this day is never far from the clicked ON person's heart. We are alive now, and that wouldn't have to be. And we are not only alive, but we are alive in this wide-open limitless universe. So being alive opens up every option in the world. And the universe is presenting each fresh moment new, awaiting the artists in us to design the day. Our artistic tools for living include our unlimited creative minds, our passionate hearts and our transcendent spirits. The day is awaiting our actions to make the connection by plugging into our aliveness socket to our right.

We can experience such a heartfelt appreciation, a gratitude for the day, for our friends and family, for our teammates and our opportunity to work. Overflowing with gratitude, the whole world feels like a well-wrapped gift.

Everyday that we become renewed with gratitude is like our birthday again, realizing we are opening up another present from life.

So, we have our unlimited creative minds in an unlimited open universe. Our only limitations are the number of creative days we have to design our destiny. And the really, really great news is that today is one of those days! It is that underlying philosophy of gratitude that greets and unites the switched ON members.

You may not believe this, but give it a try. Simply look to your right at the imaginary aliveness spirit sockets and feel your aliveness.

Plugged In – "I am ALIVE."

There are three thoughts to keep close to your heart each day:

1. We Choose Living Fully Today, Rather than Re-living Yesterday
2. We Experience Every Interaction as an Opportunity Today
3. We Feel a Sense of Urgency to Make Something Special Happen

---

1. We Choose Living Fully Today, Rather than Re-living Yesterday

Here we are. Today. What will we make of it? Each of us has about 30,000 days of life, but out of these, we have only one that we can shape now. That's today!

Each of us has to choose how we will use this valuable day- as an archeologist digging up our past, or as an architect building our future. Let's employ this precious day by living it now, rather than using this day to re-live a day from the past. We already lived out that stale day, and it is no longer accessible to shape. But here we are in this fresh, changeable day. Dwelling on what was not only drags us down, but also consumes part of our 86,400 seconds that this day offers. That's re-living! Instead let's live!

Shout to yourself a few times, "I am alive!" Feel the surge as you plug into your aliveness socket. Then tell yourself these words each day, "Today is the most important day of my life. I am going to do great things this day!"

2. **We Experience Every Interaction as an Opportunity Today**

The "hotline professionals," or the customer relation's specialists listen to the angry customer in a different way when ON. They experience the person as, not a complainer, but rather, someone frustrated with an aspect of our product or service. And the customer cared enough to take the time to call and share her frustration. No matter how upset, even angry the caller gets, the listener looks to the aliveness spirit socket on the right and stays ON. The hotline person sees this experience as an opportunity to build a long-term relationship with someone who is now upset. As they listen, they empathize, attempting to understand what the customer is experiencing and feeling.

After the customer's feelings are understood, the hotline pro then communicates an understanding of the specific problem the customer has with the product. Occasionally using the customer's name, the ON person offers understanding and reassurance, while patiently assisting the caller through her challenge. If the customer still isn't satisfied, the inspiring specialist stays focused on helping the customer through her frustrations, and her challenge. The caller is then thanked and asked to call back to share her new experience with the product. This wasn't "work," dealing with an angry customer. This was an opportunity to build a long-term customer in disguise!

Consider every interaction you have today as an opportunity to build your relationship, to inspire and encourage the other to do something great for the day, and to say "ON," rather than "OFF."

3. We Feel a Sense of Urgency to Make Something Special Happen

You can spot switched ON people immediately. How? Because their work is important, they live with a sense of urgency. Big purposes are observed in small actions. For example, they walk faster . . . because they are going places! These energizers talk with more life, more animation. Their bodies are fully engaged in their message as their eyes light up when they talk about their products and services. They love what they do, and it shows. An inspiring meeting is *crisp*, *alive*, and *to the point*. They work hard and they play hard. They are robust about their life and work. Because — what they do matters.

This sense of urgency is revealed in a "Let's get it started now!" approach to life's challenges. Getting things started now initiates our momentum and motivation. And then we are enlisting the help of Newton's Law, that is, "a body in motion tends to stay in motion." The "getting things started now" theme is especially relevant for dealing with the huge project.

When we are turned ON, we aren't intimidated by the big project. In a way, the biggest project in the world is similar to a small project. One of our young daughters suggested an interesting approach to her huge challenge while preparing for the school spelling bee. She concluded, "Hey dad, big words aren't that scary. They're just a bunch of small words put together. And if you can spell the small words, you can spell the big word."

Think about it. A seven-course meal involves making seven smaller meals, and may start off with something as simple as cracking open the first head of lettuce! In fact, some of the biggest projects in the world, from the building of the CN Tower in Toronto to the Boulder Dam (Arizona/Nevada) were a series of small projects. The huge brick building in your hometown was laid one brick at a time. Can you successfully place a brick down? If so, you can do two, five, a thousand, ten thousand. There you go!

This book, like all books, was written one word at a time. Then, one paragraph at a time. Then, one chapter at a time. Then, one book at a time. Maybe writing a book looks overwhelming. But can you write a word? Then you can write a book. There you go again!

Think about a project that you have been avoiding. Remember, when you procrastinate, for example, in cleaning your house; you do it a thousand times in your head over and over again. And, after all that mental pain, you still have to complete the project anyway, don't you?

The mood in the sparked ON community is one filled with deep respect for now because today is the only day that can be changed now. Remember: (1) choose to live today, rather than to re-live yesterday, (2) experience every interaction as an opportunity, and (3) feel a sense of urgency to make great things happen.

CHAPTER 5

OUR ATTITUDE SOCKET

Look for this socket on the wall in front of us

Our attitude is our greatest resource.

One man with courage makes a majority.

— Andrew Jackson

On the wall directly in front of you you'll discover your Attitude Spirit Socket. Like the other receptacles in your workroom, this socket is getting its power from the purpose-spirit connection generator.

The function of the attitude spirit socket is to lift our individual spirits with the awareness of the power we have, simply by the way we look at our life experiences. The attitude socket is accessible 24/7 to turn on our spirits. In fact, the best proof of the existence of our spirit is in watching its primary tool, our attitude, at work. Our attitude is the spirit tool designed to help us face challenges. And when obstacles get larger, simply dig a little deeper into your attitudinal toolbox and you'll find whatever you need to face any challenge.

The moving ON culture places a premium on the value and power of the attitude socket. We encourage you to **memorize** these three major insights, in order to help your attitude power socket burst and go to work for you — as it did to help those dozen people reach their dreams.

---

1. Its Not What Happens to Us that Affects Us; Its Our Attitude that Does
2. Our Growing Starts When Our Blaming Stops
3. We Are Our Own Sources of Inspiration Together

---

1.   Its Not What Happens That Us that Affects Us: It's Our Attitude that Does

Most of the greatest wisdom of the ages can be boiled to reawakening us to the power of our attitude socket. Two thousand years ago, the Stoic philosopher Epictetus concluded that it's not what happens to us in life that affects us, but rather it is our attitude.

This can be proven quite easily. If one hundred people all experienced the same challenging situation, would all one hundred people have the same resulting emotions to the situation and respond to it the exact way? Of course not. If one hundred people had another driver ram into the back of their car, some would get out of their car ready to get even with the "idiot," swearing and threatening for almost an hour. Imagine all of the energy the person's poor attitude has him use up. Plus he still has to deal with fixing the car!

Another driver who was hit might get out of his car, shake his head, voice his displeasure with the driver and continue for 15 minutes. (He still has the work of getting his car repaired as well). A third person might get out of his car greet the bad driver, inquire if he is "OK", get his insurance and driver's license information, and get back in his car. Five minutes: no muss, no fuss, and on his way. Done deal.

All three had experienced the same accident, yet there were three different responses. It's not what happens to us that affect us, it's our attitude that does.

Everyone in the ON community recognizes that their attitudes are more important than are their experiences. In fact, the #1 job, as they enter their workspace, is to bring in attitudes that when combined, can handle anything. They remember people in their own lives who faced the impossible with illnesses, crises, and through the right attitude overcame them. People are recalled who seemingly had everything going for them, yet spent their lives complaining.

Prove to yourself today that you can deal with anything that comes your way — without getting bent out of shape. Remember: you have the tool from your spirit — your attitude — that will help you handle challenges and crises. Be careful to make sure your attitude works for — and not against you.

2. Our Growing Starts When Our Blaming Stops

One symptom of a dispirited community is the tendency to blame others, the company, or life in general, for their circumstances. As a psychotherapist (co-author, Lewis Losoncy writing here), my eyes are constantly opened when sensing a common pattern in people who are unhappy, angry, etc. When asked why they are seeking help, patients often start by describing their symptoms and feelings. Within a few minutes they begin connecting their symptoms or feelings to someone, or something else. They then continue, piling layer upon layer of blame on the other "cause" of their unhappiness.

I might respond: that since the other person or thing was the cause of their unhappiness or anger, and then it might be better if the "real cause" came for treatment instead. Keep in mind that while the alleged reason for the patient's pain is often a relative, husband, mother-in-law, friend or boss, sometimes other "causes" might include the President, a union official, the cold winter, or even God! I then might explain that I don't know how I could get the President involved, but I could guarantee that I could heat things up for them weather wise in a few months. If the head of the union would agree, I would meet with him and reveal what they are doing to my patient. But God would be tough! After my patient stops laughing at the absurdity, I would suggest a deeper point.

Whoever or whatever we blame for why we are unhappy or angry, we make more powerful, and we put them in charge of our own emotional life. And then, we have to wait for them or it to change first for us to be happy. Guess what? That isn't going to happen.

There might be a better way. There must be a better way.

Why not accept the fact that the other person or event can never be strong enough to be the cause — since the source of our pain is our decision to empower the culprit. We don't have to continue giving our power away. It is then that we realize that when we stop blaming, we stop feeling powerless and helpless. When we stop blaming, we can start living!

The ON community lives as a non-blaming, creative culture. People are held responsible, but they are not blamed. There is a difference. Being responsible means fixing, as best we can, the error we made. Correct it and then move on. In a non-blaming culture conflicts are resolved more quickly, because people don't consume their energies defending their actions. They are held responsible to correct them.

Try living just one blame free day. Make a note about how many times in one day your energies are sapped up by getting misdirected on to a blame source, like the boss, sales, marketing, the weather, the traffic, etc. Experience your own personal growth by resisting your tendency to blame. Instead, retain your power by getting over it — and then moving swiftly from the point where you stand.

3. We Are Our Own Sources of Inspiration Together

Because motivation and spirit are high, many observers initially conclude that everyone is constantly getting praised, pats on the back, awards and never-ending positive reinforcement. Yes, these positive reinforcers occur, but they are not the key sources of inspiration. The cause of inspiration is ultimately from within, because of the person's deep sense of purpose that moves her spirits way beyond what another person can do.

It is true that people can benefit from support to go forward, to be creative, to find better ways. And that can come from the outside world. We call that praise. Praise builds extrinsically motivated people or people who are driven when someone in the outside world notices. But what if no one in the outside is present or doesn't take the time to notice? Is that an explanation for lack of motivation?

The other, longer lasting source of support, even having a more meaningful effect than praise, is encouragement. While praise focuses on successfully completed tasks, encouragement centers on noticing a person's growth, improvement and progress along the way. And while praise is someone else saying, "I like what you did, so it is good," encouragement involves getting the other person to evaluate his or her thoughts and feelings about their progress.

Encouragement is designed to nudge more inner drive — that is, to help the other person perform for the higher purpose of reaching the shared dream. And to be driven from within even without the constant need for reinforcement from others who notice and praise.

Where in your work can you move in the direction of being more inner-driven — requiring less praise and external motivation?

Remember, our attitude is our #1 resource to deal with the challenges in life. Each time we plug into the attitude socket, we go ON and see: 1) It is not what happens to us that affects us. It's the way we look at what happens that does; 2) when we stop blaming, we begin living; and (3) when we are driven from within, we are guaranteed that we will reach it. After all we are the driving force.

CHAPTER 6

OUR ASSET SOCKET

Look for this socket on the wall to our left

> *We are moving from our strengths.*
>
> *We can't pick people up,*
> *by putting them down*
>
> *– Lewis Losoncy*

The first spirit power receptacle is our aliveness socket in which we reconnect to the realization that we are alive. A wall away, in front of us, is our attitude socket that offers the power to turn us ON to understand our view of things is stronger than our circumstances. On the third wall, to our left, we find our asset socket. Our asset socket gives us the spark by focusing on our strengths. This third receptacle is designed to help us see more clearly what's right rather than what's wrong. Look for the assets, resources, and possibilities, rather than dwelling on the deficiencies, liabilities and weaknesses.

The greatest discovery from the field of psychology was to shift the focus from what's wrong with a person, towards centering on what's right with that same person. For over a century, psychologists were looking in all the wrong places to help people. Previously influenced by our understandings gathered from observing very seriously disturbed people, à la Sigmund Freud, psychologists concluded that it was nearly impossible for a person to change. And then, as a result of, believe it or not, studies on rats, pigeons and earthworms, à la B.F. Skinner, psychologists argued we were helpless products of our past conditioning.

It was through optimistic psychiatrist Alfred Adler that we realized our creative human power. Adler asserted that it was neither heredity nor environment that shaped us- they are only the building blocks out of which we create ourselves. And more recently, Martin Seligman found the empowering field of Positive Psychology, which emphasizes focusing on our strengths. People who plug into their asset socket for strength agree.

In this chapter we center on two insights to bring to the workplace each day. First, whatever we focus on, grows. Second, let's put our best foot forward.

---

1. Whatever We Focus on Grows. Let's Center on The Positive
2. Let's Put Our Best Foot Forward

---

1. Whatever We Focus On Grows. Let's Center On the Positive

Someone once wrote, "Two men looked out from jailhouse bars. One saw mud, One saw stars!"

Whether we are aware of it or not, we have a bias as we approach each day. For example, a "down" person comes into life experiences with a predisposition to quickly hone in on all of the problems and difficulties. A "more positive" person arrives at the same events and is biased toward seeing both what are right with the situation, and what opportunities it presents to them.

As you look around the room you are in, choose to center in on a certain color, let's say white. Look around for everything that is white. You'll soon be seeing more and more white, as the other colors start fading into the background.

Now change the color that you are focusing on to red. Center on your new color and observe what happens. You'll soon see more and more red appearing. And white starts disappearing into the background!

Whatever we focus on, will grow.

Whatever We Focus on Grows

. . . .

💡 TURNING IT ON

"Take This Job and Shove It!"

Try this experiment. Take a few minutes and create an argument for why your job is the worst in the world. As you really dig into it, live it, experience all of the boring and frustrating parts, the impossible circumstances, and the difficult people. Then, reflect for a minute or two on the negative aspects of your work.

As you centered on all of the challenges and frustrating parts of your work, how were you feeling about your work?

. . . .

By focusing in on what's wrong, you probably began to see more and more of the negative — and perhaps this created more frustration, more negative feelings, maybe even depression or anger! Whatever we focus on grows.

. . . .

🔆 TURNING IT ON

"I Love My Work!"

Now, try another experiment. Take a few minutes or so to create an argument for why your work is the best in the world. Think about all of the rewards, the joys, the teamwork, the products, the successes and every other positive aspect of your work. Reflect for a few minutes on the positive aspects of your work.

Did you create, inside yourself, different feelings about your work?

· ·

Imagine how much energies are spent dwelling on the negative aspects of our work — creating more and more misery for ourselves. And the one who is affected the most by choosing a negative spin at work is the one who is spinning! Center on what's right — and then, more and more good news starts appearing!

2.   Let's Put Our Best Foot Forward

Sometimes a talented person is not working in a position that utilizes their strengths to the max. This can be frustrating to the person who has so much more to contribute to a project, team or department. For example, the person who loves precision might be more comfortable working with the final details of the product, rather than in the brainstorming phases of its development. Or another person who loves going out on the limb and taking risks might work well creatively, pushing the limits of ideas. That person wouldn't sit well, or perform well, with "numbers crunchers."

The outgoing, people-loving community member needs to be with people, and her best contributions might be in sales. The introvert might love working with the screen, researching ideas to help the team to reach its purpose — (the why?). The nitpicker is the perfect person to take a microscope to every nook and cranny in the safety department, in an attempt to lower accidents and the resultant insurance rates. Is stubbornness a negative trait? I think we all would like our heart surgeon to have a stubborn determination to be perfect. Wouldn't we?   How could a stubborn person's assets best be used in a workspace?

The optimist could offer a sales force hope and determination, while the realist is just as necessary in analyzing product performance.

Commit to putting the pieces of the people performance puzzle together in the most fitting way. Are you in the right fit?

. . . .

☀ TURNING IT ON

Where is your best fit?

- What are your best talents and skills?

- What gives you the most satisfaction in your work?

- Combining your best talents, skills and satisfaction, where would you ideally fit into your work community?

. . . .

Realize that whatever you choose to center on, will grow. So, center on the positive. Then move forward lifted by your strengths.

CHAPTER 7

OUR ACCEPTANCE SOCKET

Look for this socket on the wall behind us

> *What is, Is!*
>
> *– Lewis Losoncy*
>
> *Acceptance of what has happened is the first step to overcoming the consequences of any misfortune.*
>
> *– William James*

The socket on the wall to our right has the energy to turn us on to our life. On the wall in front of us we gain enlightenment from our attitude that offers us the power to light up the darkest night. And from the wall on the left we receive strengths from realizing our assets and potentials. The fourth wall in the room offers us a socket to serenity. This is directly in back of us and is often not noticed due to its location.

This part of our workspace is a bit different. Near the acceptance socket, we place the lamp with the most relaxing light on our coffee table. The acceptance wall allows us to meditate, relax, and find serenity and peace sprinkled with doses of humor. Our humor is founded in accepting our shortcomings, fallibilities, sometime delusions, and our overall humanness.

When ON, we don't deny tough realities, but actually become enlightened in a different way by facing challenges with extreme doses of acceptance and humor.

---

1. We Immediately Accept What We Aren't Going to Change
2. We Grow from Every Experience, Good or Bad
3. We Use Humor to Handle Challenges

---

1.   We Immediately Accept What We Aren't Going to Change

So much energy is consumed by people who can't get over a setback, and dig a deeper ditch of frustration, dwelling on what should be, rather than what — in reality — is. People switched ON remember the fourth wall in the workspace has the answers in the face of the impossible. Acceptance! Letting go.

When ON, we don't lose a step when a project fails, or when a stop sign appears or we lose a big customer. Instead we immediately accept what can't be changed, or what we choose not to change. And this ability to adjust to the new reality is immediately therapeutic. Since there is nothing that can be done to change the circumstances, start from the new reality, and lay the past to rest.

The mantra is "What is, is!" If there is a power outage on the big day of the release of the fall line occurs, should the outage have happened?

Yes, of course. Why? Because it did! What is, is!

If it is ninety degrees outside and it's snowing, should it be snowing? Yes! Why? Because it is!

What is, Is!

. . . .

🔆 TURNING IT ON

Prove to Yourself That You Can "Get Over It!"

What do you need to accept so that you can get over it? Develop your ability to accept what you aren't going to change. Keep reminding yourself, "What is, is!"

. . . .

🔆 TURNING IT ON

Encourage Your Teammates to "Get Over It!"

What does your work team or company need to accept and get over? How can you help to bring a "What is, is!" insight into the community? Remember you can be an inspiring therapeutic healing source for your team.

. . . .

2. We Grow from Every Experience, Good or Bad

After losing its dynamic founder and leader, every one in the company comes together to re-new its purpose. Each person makes a commitment to carry on the founder's dream — which has now become their own. Imagine if this same community was formerly prone to hand wringing and developing feelings of collective hopelessness. Or, what if their "way of being" was to start ruminating — thinking negative thought after negative thought? Such a loss could have ignited a downhill direction for the community.

Instead, the reality of the loss was appropriately grieved and accepted. The inspiring community then turned ON, kicking their creative determination into drive. They developed new ideas built upon the founder's principles. The realization soon emerged that if they could survive their most challenging loss, through their ideas, products and purpose (the why?) they have the strength and resources to carry "ON" the important work.

If they can make it under these overwhelming challenging circumstances, they have the ability to handle virtually anything.

3.   We Use Humor to Handle Challenges

People who are turned ON typically use humor in their day-to-day work. Making use of a sense of humor helps to re-route frustration in challenging times and is based on the awareness that we do not take things personally. Consider the history of people taking their life experiences personally.

Originally, people thought that the sun revolved around the earth and the earth was the center of the solar system. Then we found that we were not at the center, because our earth was actually revolving around the sun. This humiliating insight was so tough to take that many frustrated people developed a new theory of the universe. They began believing that the universe revolved around them personally! Sure. We all know this. It is called "egocentrism."

Have you ever met any of these ego-centrists — people who think that universal and earthly events revolve around them personally? You can observe them wherever you go. They stand out from the crowd, believing that the universe is choosing to signal them out and frustrate them. Red lights, traffic jams, weather conditions, long lines in banks and supermarkets, IRS audits, and running out of gas far away from life, all are just a few of the events that can bring them down. It's as if they are saying, "These annoyances should happen to others, but not to someone like me!"

Now most of us are only rarely guilty of being egocentrics. It is most evidenced in those moments when we are using the words, "should," or "shouldn't" to describe how the universe *should* rearrange our experiences in ways more favorable for us. It's unlikely that in the real world the so-called "shoulds" of millions of people actually causes things to happen. It is more likely that the "is!" in life is reality. ("What is, is!" represents the real world.) There are no "shoulds" and "shouldn'ts," in the universe's vocabulary. If so, where do these words come from?

Well, if we were running the universe (and most of us think we "should" be, "shouldn't" we?) our "shoulds" are the way we would design things. Unfortunately, we are in a lesser position and have to accept, "what is!" rather than what we think it "should" be.

The average person uses hundreds of "shoulds" every day — many of them in their workspace. And every time we say the word "should," at that moment, we are creating frustration for ourselves. When hearing yourself getting "shouldy," simply turn around and look at the acceptance spirit socket on wall to your back and plug in. When plugged into our acceptance socket, we have the power to remind ourselves and others: "Since it is not likely that the universe is attacking us personally, let's simply realize that "what is, is!" and ask ourselves instead, "what's our plan?"

Lighten up. Don't take things so personally. And instead, find humor when you start hearing your "shoulds," to realize that the snowstorm was not a personal event! In a short period of time and practice, you'll find yourself laughing at things that once drove you up a tree! Just look around for the spirit socket power in back of you. If you are driving, do this mentally, please. It will still work.

In our own ON community, we occasionally notice someone spinning their arms around their head reminding their teammates that we are acting as if the universe is rotating around us personally by sending these inconveniences!

. . . .

💡 TURNING IT ON

What do you think shouldn't be?

Why shouldn't it be?

Considering the facts that what it should or shouldn't be doesn't because "what is is," what's your plan!

. . . .

Remember, immediately accept anything you aren't going to change, realize that you can grow from every experience, good or bad, and use humor to lighten things up!

What is, is!

CHAPTER 8

OUR ANSWERS SOCKET

This socket is on the ceiling, in the center

Our challenges have solutions.

Quite often you will find your own greatness by saying, 'Yes' while others are saying, 'No.'

– Colin Walsh

In the attitude room of our life, each of the four walls has a socket to connect to — that can give us the power to turn our motivational lights ON. To the right is our aliveness spirit socket that we plug into to remind ourselves that we are alive and that today is our moment to make things happen. In front of us is our attitude spirit socket that provides us strength to keep realizing that the things that happen to us don't affect us — its our attitude that does. To our left is our asset socket that gives us the power to center on our strengths, our accomplishments and our possibilities. And at our back, right behind us on the floor, is our acceptance socket that gives us the energy to find serenity, peace and even humor in challenging times that we cannot change. When we look at that socket, it is shouting to us, "What is, is!"

Now look up to find the fifth socket. Here you gain your fifth power to stay ON. In the center of the ceiling is our "Answers Spirit Socket" — the receptacle that offers us the power to proceed with the knowledge that if we turn ON our light, we can eventually overcome the darkness of any challenge. Think about this: That's why, when you observe optimists looking for answers, their eyes are peering up.

More than anything else, the turned ON community is inspired by an unbending optimistic conviction that "there is a way!" This belief gives them the motivation to find the way using their creative determination. There are three underlying themes of optimism present.

---

1. We Proceed as If Challenges Have Solutions
2. We Are Could-be-ness Thinkers
3. We Are Determined to Find a Way

---

1.   We Proceed as If Challenges Have Solutions

When speaking to an Ohio graduating class, we asked the new grads, "Who in here believes we can cure the world's hunger problems in the next five years?" No one raised a hand!

We then responded, "That's why we won't! What if just one of you would have raised your hand and said, 'Yes!' And then another optimist might have added to the first idea, then another, and another. We would be on our way — All because one person initiated a momentum with a 'Yes!'"

The power of optimism!

The philosopher Bertrand Russell asserted, "In the vast realm of the alive, creative human mind, there are no limitations." Whether we find solutions for challenges or not, starts with a belief, upfront — that there is an answer somewhere in our creative minds.

Off: "*I see the sun isn't out today.*"
On: "*Just look above the clouds.*"

Think about how a predisposed mindset of optimism works when facing crises. Picture the typical light switch with an "ON" and "OFF" side. Imagine entering a dark, empty house at night and deciding to walk randomly around searching without any light for one specific room.

Or, you can turn the light ON and proceed more directly and more quickly to your goal. When facing a challenge, before drifting into the dark, believing there are no answers, quickly think of that light switch; enlighten yourself to proceed as if there is an answer. Plug into the answers socket on the floor in the center of the room. Turn your mindset to the "Yes, there is an answer" switch.

Remind each other of times in the past, when you faced problems, and turned to the "Yes, there is a way!" -- giving yourself the enlightening drive to solve the problem.

2.   We Are Could-Be-Ness Thinkers

The switched ON is inspired by another way they look at life. While many people are narrow, literal thinkers, in an inspiring culture, things are viewed from its "could-be-ness." For example, a narrow thinker experiences a pencil as just something to write with. The could-be-ness thinker adds value to everything by being aware that things can be so much more than they appear when moving from the robotic mode.

When thinking about the truer value of their products and services, could-be-ness thinkers see so much more than someone who just continues to see things the way they always saw them. And imagine the could-be-ness thinking real estate agent who walks into a new home and brings to life the scent of the fireplace — its crackling sounds and the flickering reflections over the oaken floor on a snowy January evening! This could-be-ness thinker sees more, feels more and adds more value to everything they focus on.

. . . .

🔆 TURNING IT ON

Becoming a Could-Be-Ness Thinker

Take a simple object around you. Any object, a cup, a piece of paper, a chair. Brainstorm. Let every idea emerge, no matter how crazy or far out it might at appear at first. Proceed until you have 20 ways you can think about or use that object. Take as long as you need.

1.
2.
3.
4.
5.
6.
7.
8.
9.
10.
11.
12.
13.
14.
15.
16.
17.
18.
19.
20.

. . . .

3.   We Are Determined to Find a Way

Creative determination is one of the most obvious themes observed in the ON community.

The belief and the willingness to find a way initiates the world-changing process. Every great achievement in the world was accomplished by "find-awayers!" The placing of the flag on the moon, the curing of diseases, the building of great countries, the success of successful businesses, the extra winning effort of champion sports teams. All found a way!

This creative determination combines using your unlimited could-be-ness thinking mind with your stubborn refusal to give up. — To say, "ON," rather than "OFF," even when standing against all odds. Keep reminding each other to stay in the brainstorming mode, creatively offering and accepting every alternative, unblocked by fears, anxieties, threats, or criticisms. Open the doors to let all of the ideas in and to grow. Let the ideas flow, and we will find better ways. And remember, partial answers are treasured as well.

Proceed as if your challenges have solutions, and think could-be-ness thoughts and be stubbornly determined to find a way.

PART III

HIT THE "ON" SWITCH

8 Electric Lights to Turn ON Our Workplace

Electrifying

Loving

Encouraging

Connecting

Trusting

Respecting

Inspiring

Celebrating

The previous five spirit-sockets offered us power to keep our spirits energized in our workspaces. Simply plug into the lift you need by looking for the appropriate spirit socket. The inspiring community treasures the energy and potential in each day — in fact in each moment. They value the importance of their attitude, focus on their strengths, immediately accept the things they can't change, and precede with an unbending optimism that "We can do it!"

In addition to these five power or spirit-sockets, we also have eight electric ways to turn others ON to their work.

In this part of the book, we present these eight inspiring, helpful ways of interacting with others to encourage a climate of growth and motivation to develop new ideas and better ways.

Electrifying involves adding life and energy by enthusiastically communicating upbeat thoughts, messages and ideas to turn our workspaces ON.

Loving involves revering the community, customer, products and services to add value to our daily lifework.

Encouraging is occurring when we are highlighting another's strengths, while seeing their higher possibilities.

We are using the **connecting** approach when we are relating to another person how he or she "fits in" and belongs in the community.

Trusting involves communicating belief and confidence in another community member.

We are **respecting** when we are taking the time to understand, and to find worth in each person's unique role, with its responsibilities, joys, challenges, frustrations and conflicts.

Inspiring is a way of motivating others by reminding them of the human significance of their work — and how they are making the world a better place.

We are employing the strategy of **celebrating** when we are recognizing a person's efforts, improvements and progress.

CHAPTER 9

ELECTRIFYING:

"Life-ing" things up with positive communications.

> *Win tonight, and we will walk together forever!*
>
> *— Fred Shero,*
> *Coach of the Broad Street Bullies*
> *(aka Philadelphia Flyers) —*
> *Stanley Cup Champs, 1974*

We all know the electrifier. We enjoy being with him or her because we start "coming to life" in this person's presence. The electrifier's vocabulary is filled with positive, energizing words, and even problems are perceived as invigorating challenges. While to the "downer," a setback is viewed as a catastrophe, to an electrifier, the same setback is a mere inconvenience — with a long-term opportunity.

The electrifier knows that words shape emotions, and emotions shape actions (or inactions). Words are biochemical triggers that signal our body's motivation to go forward in anticipation of success — or to retreat in fear. While the downer vocabulary is replete with energy consuming words, like "can't," "rut," "overwhelmed," "problems," "shoulds," and "shouldn'ts," the upbeat energizer has a crisp, on the move, uplifting vocabulary emphasizing "can" over "can't," "new" over "old," and filled with phrases expressing exciting, youthful, fresh, revealing opportunity and hope.

Sense how the downers and electrifiers experience the same circumstances:

Downer	Electrifier
"Things look bad for us."	"We face an exciting opportunity."
"We missed our goal by 2%."	"We reached 98% of our goals. Congratulations!"
"Maybe it can be done."	"It absolutely can be done. And we are the ones who can do it."
"We are not as young as we used to be"	"We will never be younger than we are today. And we never had more wisdom than

we do today. This is our time."

"Our team is too small to
take on that job."

"The quality of the people
we have here make us the
logical choice to take on that
job."

---

1. Positive Environmental Engineering
2. The Electrifying People In The Work Environment
3. Electrifying the Physical Environment

---

1. Positive Environmental Engineering

Many psychologists have concluded that we are products of our environments, but often forget that our environments are also products of us!

The switched ON team encourages every one to become a positive environmental engineer, designing and building a more uplifting, energizing, life-giving environment to work within. An unstimulating, drab — or worse yet, a cynical, sarcastic or negative environment, is unlikely going to give us the spark of energy we need to find-a-way.

There are two vital influencing factors in our environment, the (1) people part, and (2) the physical part.

2. The Electrifying People in the Work Environment

Just as the food we eat affects our bodies, the people whose ideas we listen to affects our thinking. So, never get advice from someone who hasn't achieved what you'd like to achieve. If you wonder whether something can be done or not, ask someone who has done it before. Chances are good that the person will tell you it can be done, energizing you with the courage and desire to go forward.

Make it unfashionable to be a downer. Inspiration doesn't survive in an energy-sapping context. This doesn't mean that tough realities are denied and not faced. Later in this book, we will experience how challenges are addressed head-on in an inspiring culture.

The electrifier always has a positive spin on a setback. After all, inspiration stems from our spirit, and our inner spirit is stronger than our outer circumstances. Earlier we defined our spirit as our unlimited resource that transcends, and adds strength to our weary physical bodies and fragile psychological egos. When our bodies and minds are down, an insight from our spirits give us the jolt!

The first way of energizing our work environment is by inspiring the development of a culture of people who are filled with energy, hope and positive motivation. Each person moves from the highest part of his or her mind, heart and spirit.

. . . .

💡 TURNING IT ON

View Yourself as a Motivational Speaker for your Department

Develop a one-minute inspirational and motivational speech to give to everyone in your department. You might consider packaging past achievements and potential future accomplishments. Add any other special aspects of your team of which you are proud. Give special recognition for team members who energize the team.

. . . .

3. Electrifying The Physical Environment

The community's spirits can be energized, not only by the people who are part of the environment, but also by the physical environment as well. An uplifting environment is one that gives the team a constant upbeat "talk," encouraging the team to keep a plugging- away attitude at their important work, while providing for their needs of stimulation, relaxation and inspiration. Advertisers spend millions of dollars on jingles, phrases, colors, sights and sounds to effectively influence buying habits. Why? Because it works! Creating a stimulating, find-a-way environment can inspire people to keep on, even against all odds.

Some companies take their employees away from the workplace, to an offsite hotel or retreat setting for their training program. Yet they return to the same old work environment. Imagine energizing your own workplace with positive stimulation and meaningful reasons to change the world from within your own worksite. Encourage everyone to bring in quotes that inspire them personally and post them at a special spot in your environment. You could also "engineer up" your workplace by developing your own advertising campaign.

. . . .

☀ TURNING IT ON

Develop an Advertising Campaign
Shouting the Great News about Your Department

Start an advertising campaign with themes about your department's mission, claims-to-fames and success. Post the theme at various locations, to keep reminding each other about their important work and stoke the fires of their creative determination

. . . .

CHAPTER 10

LOVING:

Revering our community, customer, products and services

> *Happiness is the world's greatest renewable resource, because no matter how much you share with others, you will never run out.*
>
> *– Colin Walsh*

---

1. Loving Our Customers
2. Loving Our Products and Services

---

1.   Loving Our Customers

There was a revolution brewing in the early 80's in the professional beauty manufacturing business. A passionate hairdresser from Beechwood, Ohio, Arnie Miller, who with his wife Sydell, changed an industry. Arnie loved and was extremely proud of his profession. He would boast at parties attended by attorneys or physicians that, "I'm a hairdresser!" And he wanted every hairdresser in the world to experience his same proud feelings about their work. So he created a company that allowed them to realize their dreams.

Arnie dreamt of elevating his profession even before he had produced his first product. As he traveled to every imaginable US and Canadian city, speaking with sincere love about the important work of hairdressers throughout the world, he quickly accumulated a following. At the end of his speeches, he let the hairdressers know that he had designed professional products for those who were interested. In less than a decade, Arnie and Sydell's company became the leader, and remains the leader today influencing hairdressers throughout the world with the message, "Love your work, fellow hairdressers. Your work changes the world."

Like Arnie Miller, let's learn to love our community and our customers!

. . . .

 **TURNING IT ON**

Loving Our Customers

If you have direct contact with customers, describe your relationship with your favorite person and why he or she is the most special one to you.

_____

_____

_____

_____

_____

_____

_____

_____

_____

. . . .

2. Loving Our Products and Services

You've experienced people who could romance their work, by seeing so much more in their every day jobs than others, who are just going through the motions in the workplace.

Terry Tears is a Melbourne, Florida carpenter. The best I've ever met. He is an artist, a scientist, and a perfectionist with wood. From mahogany to pine, he not only knows wood — like his neighbor Tim Wakefield knows the knuckleball — he loves wood like Mother Theresa loved people. When a thrilled customer once observed, "Terry you could have done anything you wanted to with your life," Terry smiled and responded, "I know, and that's exactly what I am doing!" Terry loves wood! He is a perfect example of someone who loves his products and services.

Gene Budgeon, the pest control specialist would greet you with his card, "Gene Budgeon, your bug man!" He knew everything about pest control and was extremely passionate about his work. He once looked up at the telephone wires stretched across our yard, and saw a falcon staring down at its prey — ready to pounce — and reassured us: "We are working together to get rid of these pests for you!" Nothing felt better for Gene than when your house was finally bug free. He took the mission personally, because he loved his work. What he did for a living was important. His customers slept well at night. Gene offered reassurance and security to thousands during his reign as the bug king.

Speaking of everyday heroes, very few can top Chris Cohill, dynamic oyster schucker at Lobster Shanty in Fenwick Island, Delaware. After decades of schuckin, he still loves both his work — but especially oysters. Chris understands each one's unique personality, where it came from, how challenging it will be to open and how sweet it will taste. You could say that Chris has found the answer to making the most of his life at work. He has gained the respect of the whole community of consumers who utilize his services.

. . . .

🔆 TURNING IT ON

Loving Our Products and Services

What do you love most about your work, your products and services?

_____

_____

_____

_____

_____

_____

_____

. . . .

CHAPTER 11

ENCOURAGING:

Highlighting strengths, resources and possibilities

> *The great leaders are like the best conductors –*
> *they reach beyond the notes to reach*
> *the magic in the players.*
>
> *– Blaine Lee*

The next time you are with a group of people, look for the encourager. This is the person whose arrival lights up the atmosphere, who circulates good news and conveys the energy-giving hope that raises the "will" over the "won't." The encouraging person is buoyed up with the advantage of being positive, of being certain that life is worth living, that people would rather hope than despair, and that fear is the only enemy we face in life.

The antidote to fear is courage. And this courage is produced by encouragement.

Ultimately, the encouraging person's gift is a positive attitude coupled with the skills to encourage others to realize their strengths. And even beyond these strengths, they have resources that may be hidden — even to them. These same assets are noticed and unearthed to the encourager, who has a deeper vision as to where the person's gold is buried. The encourager also makes the connections between the strengths, the hidden resources and a person's possibilities and potential.

. . . .

☀ TURNING IT ON

Success Strength Training!

Make a list of everyone in your immediate community. Take a few minutes to encourage each one, by identifying each person's strengths —- whether technical or personal. (Example of strengths: "You are the best at working with our customers." "You are really talented artistically." "You keep things loose around here.")

Person	3 Strengths
1. _____	1. _____ 2. _____ 3. _____
2. _____	1. _____ 2. _____ 3. _____
3. _____	1. _____ 2. _____ 3. _____
4. _____	1. _____ 2. _____ 3. _____
5. _____	1. _____ 2. _____ 3. _____
6. _____	1. _____ 2. _____ 3. _____
7. _____	1. _____ 2. _____ 3. _____
8. _____	1. _____ 2. _____ 3. _____
9. _____	1. _____ 2. _____ 3. _____
10. _____	1. _____ 2. _____ 3. _____

When you all get together with your lists, gather in a circle or around a table, and focus on one person at a time — and experience "Success Strength Training!"

. . . .

More than anything else, the turned ON community is an inspiring, positive place of encouragement. The strengths that a person brings to the office, mill, hospital, classroom, or on the road are not only noticed with one's extended antennae, looking for potential, they are also developed even more in that growing atmosphere.

CHAPTER 12

CONNECTING:

Relating how a person belongs, and fits in

No you are not too old at 70. I'm not going to let you quit Frank. When you are here in our plant, the mood changes.
Besides picking people up at the airport, we need you to just walk around and lift our spirits. Now get back to work!

– Syd, GM, Plywood Factory

Experiencing oneself as a contributor in some way, shape, or form connects us to our larger community. Its how we "fit in." In fact, the renowned psychiatrist Alfred Adler argued that our social needs are the most important needs we have. These are our needs for attention, belonging and contributing. If we don't get attention for doing the right thing, we can get attention by doing the wrong thing. If we don't fit in with our positive behaviors, we will fit in — by getting noticed — with our rebellious actions. We strive for a role, to find our place, positive or negative, in our social community.

Our experiences suggest that many individuals quit their jobs because of people reasons, stresses with others or just because they feel that they don't fit in. Some people fit in by bringing humor to lighten things up. Others are good at being able to smooth over stressful relationships. Others as good teachers, great customer specialists, skilled technicians, and even great snack bringers!

Looks like you are going to fit in here perfectly, Norton.

Our friend Glenn Parker has written a insightful, and practical book, *Team Players and Teamwork,* in which he outlines four types of roles team players play on their work teams. They include (1) the contributor or task-centered person, (2) the collaborator or goal-centered teammate, (3) the communicator or the people person and (4) the challenger or the questioner.

---

1. The Contributor Style and How Contributors Inspire
2. The Collaborator Style and How Collaborators Inspire
3. The Communicator Style and How Communicators Inspire
4. The Challenger Style and How Challengers Inspire

---

1.   The Contributor Style and How Contributors Inspire

Love the contributors. They are focused on the task at hand. Contributors inspire by getting their job done, on time. They are specialists. You can count on the contributor.

Focused on the job they need to get done, contributors see their roles as providing the group with the best possible information. In the contributor's view, effective team problem solving and decision-making result from the sharing of each team member's expertise. The contributor tends to view a team as a group of experts in their specific areas, and everyone should be able to have their work completed efficiently and effectively on time.

Contributors have high standards for their work and expect the same of their teammates. Contributors use words like "quality," "excellence" and "results" to describe their expectations. "Tell me what to do within my area of expertise and skill, and the task will be completed -- and on time," is the contributor's message.

Contributors inspire the community by getting their part of the job done effectively and on time. They are great role models for achievement.

2. The Collaborator Style and How Collaborators Inspire

You also have to love the collaborator on your team. Unlike the contributor who focuses in on specific tasks, the collaborator is the big picture person who centers on the whole goal. Being goal directed players, collaborators keep their eye on the vision. The collaborator is constantly reminding the team to stay on track and to keep focused on the bull's eye.

Unlike the contributor, collaborators eagerly will work outside their area of expertise to get things done. And while a contributor might say, "That's not my job," collaborators roll up their sleeves and keep their eyes on the goal line. If they were on a one-mile relay track team, they'd start, run second, third or anchor, whatever will help the team win. On a baseball team, while the contributor might be the home run hitting first baseman that will get their specific job done, a collaborator or the utility player who will play any position, even pitch if needed!

Collaborators are proud of their team, and find it easy to give credit.

Collaborators derive satisfaction from being a part of a successful team, more than they do giving their own individual effort. They realize that their contributions are necessary for the team's success, but they do not require individual recognition to be satisfied with their work. Collaborating team players focus on what's good for the company — not just what's good for their department.

Collaborators inspire by keeping the team focused on the big purpose, (the why?) and by chipping in wherever and whenever needed, even if they have to get out of their own area of expertise to get the whole job done.

3. The Communicator Style and How Communicators Inspire

Everyone also loves the communicator for their warm personal style — offering empathy, encouragement and support. The communicator is the people person on the team who is interested in the interactions among people. While the contributor is centering in on the task, and the collaborator is looking at the goal, the communicator is helping the other two to find a middle ground that they both can agree on.

Communicators have a knack of knowing what is needed on the team. After all, since people are what teams are all about, communicators are those who put energy on the people on the team. Communicators know when to bring in the out, and lift up the down. Communicators provide for a very important function on the team process bringing the glue to cement relationships together.

Communicators inspire the team through their sensitivity to the "people parts." When someone feels left out, it is the communicator who brings the person back into the fold. Communicators help to resolve conflicts and spot morale problems long before they actively surface. At meetings they bring out the ideas from the more docile members and are always there to encourage and support their teammates.

4. The Challenger Style and How Challengers Inspire

After thinking things through, the challenger eventually gains respect. Some team members are uncomfortable around the challenger because the challenger calls it as she sees it. Challengers are direct and frank, sometimes confronting, because they, like the other team members are deeply concerned about the team. They very much want the team to succeed. However, challengers may appear to be a negative force on the team, since they often express opposition to the prevailing thought.

Glenn Parker reveals in *Team Players and Teamwork*, that a challenger wants to know why the team is doing things a certain way, and if that's the best way. These questioners will point out inconsistencies in the team's words and actions and can argue in favor of a customer if service, for example, was down. If the team isn't living up to its purpose (the why?), the challenger surfaces to get the team back on course.

The challenger may make other team members feel uncomfortable. If the team isn't living up to its tasks and goals, it is the challenger who rises up, and points it out. The challenger also is a highly ethical person who encourages the team to set higher standards for their work.

You can imagine the interplay of the challenger's "questioning things style" with the sensitive communicator. Challengers sometimes feel that communicators are too soft. Communicators cringe at the harder approach of the challenger.

Challengers don't want to be bound by the past and are open to trying new ideas and then evaluate them analytically.

Challengers inspire by calling into question the team's shortcomings, and are the only ones who are often strong enough to confront the team, when it strays from or lost its purpose (the why?)

· ·

TURNING IT ON

What's Your Style?

Considering the Contributor (Focused on the Task), the Collaborator (Centered on the Whole Picture), the Communicator (the People Person) and the Challenger (the Questioner). Which style describes you most accurately? Why?

How could you better relate with and inspire the other three types?

1.

2.

3.

. . . .

CHAPTER 13

TRUSTING:

Communicating belief and confidence

Belief is the best preparation for getting results.

— Colin Walsh

The poet Goethe observed, "If you want someone to develop a trait, treat them as though they already have it." One of the best predictors of an individual or a team's performance is their expectations. Theodore Roosevelt concluded that if you believe you can you were half way there. Winning teams expect to win. Losing teams aren't sure. Research in education provides support for the idea that if a teacher believes in a student and expects the student to do well, her belief communicates confidence which plays a role in influencing the student's own positive expectations.

Think about it for a moment. If someone believes in us and communicates that confidence, along with a belief that our work is important, we will have a tendency to take a renewed look at ourselves. Deep down we may hope the person is right, so we try to prove the trusting person right. The fact that some psychologists tell us we only use about 10% of our potential demonstrates that there is always room for improvement. And the cause of this improvement may be someone's trust that communicates belief and confidence.

Further support for the role of belief and confidence comes from the field of medicine. In the book *Persuasion and Healing*, Jerome Frank discussed the power of the doctor's expectations on the patient's cure. Numerous studies describe the effects of the placebo, or sugar pill, combined with guarantees from the doctor that, "This pill will get rid of your symptoms." By communicating positive expectations, the doctor can influence the patient's attitude, energy, health and outcome.

In *Anatomy of an Illness*, the popular writer Norman Cousins was told that he had a disease that had never been cured before. How's that for creating hopeless expectations and a downhill feeling? Norman was fortunate enough to find a doctor who offered positive expectations and a sense of hope. The physician's positive beliefs empowered the writer onward to search for the cure.

Cousins concluded that if negative expectations and negative thinking in a negative environment could produce symptoms of diseases, why couldn't the reverse be true? Could surrounding yourself with a positive environment lead to good health? He started what he called, "the laughing cure," which involved watching reruns of funny movies creating a laugh-inviting environment. The writer invited his comedian friends in to the hospital to share their humor. He checked out of the hospital concluding, "A hospital is no place for a sick person." Norman Cousins was eventually cured of his "incurable," disease. All of his motivation to go forward started as a result of a doctor who believed in him.

The switched ON culture is one of trust, belief, confidence and positive expectations. Why not? If after focusing in on strengths, resources and potential to achieve an important purpose, and after earning support and respect from others, the community moves forward together propelled by the powers of trusting and believing.

. . . .

🔆 TURNING IT ON

The Power of Belief!

Who believed in you in your workplace? Cite an example when this person communicated his or her belief. And how did you feel when he or she communicated belief in you?

_____

_____

_____

_____

_____

_____

_____

_____

. . . .

. . . .

💡 TURNING IT ON

You Gotta Believe!

Who do you believe in at your workplace? Why do you believe in this person? Share with the person your observations about his or her abilities.

_____

_____

_____

_____

_____

_____

_____

_____

. . . .

CHAPTER 14

RESPECTING:

Valuing each person's unique roles and responsibilities

> *If you have some respect for people as they are, you can be more effective in helping them to become better than they are.*
>
> *— John W. Gardner*

Perhaps you've seen a picture, similar to the one we recently encountered — the theme of observing the world through the eyes of a New Yorker. Ninety per cent of the illustration was about New York, including the Empire State Building, Yankee Stadium, the Theatre District, Times Square, and all the standard New York landmarks. The remaining 10% embraced the balance of the world, including the Atlantic Ocean, a smaller Pacific Ocean, a tiny China, a missing New Zealand, an Eiffel Tower that comprised most of Europe, and a hint of South America. One could make a map from the eyes of any other city dweller and, of course, there would be a disproportionate emphasis on one's hometown.

The same is true in our workplace. There tends to exist a similar natural myopia related to our own unique roles and responsibilities. We understand, and oftentimes overestimate the challenges and frustrations of our own roles that we intimately experience each workday. It can be quite invigorating, when someone outside our department takes the time to communicate her grasp and respect for our job — can't it?

The World Through the Eyes of A Dentist

For example, the enthusiastic sales manager speaks to her counterpart in the creative department. "All of us in sales really appreciate and respect your efforts in marketing, and realize the short deadline you faced to create this promo. We know the constant pressure on you guys, yet you come through every time!"

Or consider the young man in packaging who wanders into the HR office sharing, "I really admire what you guys have to do to keep this company afloat. During these tough times, it can't be easy for you, since you are being asked to do all these different

111

things, while helping with everyone's personal and professional problems. I just wanted you to know that someone out here thinks about the stress you face here in HR!"

While somewhat rare, understanding another person's world can be a very therapeutic experience, for both parties. The more you walk a mile in the shoes of someone from a different department, the more appreciation you gain for them. And the more you understand that they too have stresses and challenges, the more sensitive you become towards their situation and the less resentful you feel towards them. This eases conflicts between departments, and even helps create better ways to make each other's lives more productive.

Most people in a community are intimately aware of the unique stresses, pressures, frustrations and demands they face. On a baseball team, for example, pitchers look at what is important on the diamond differently than the position players do. In fact, many great hitters hated pitchers, even their own teammates. The legendary Red Sox slugger, Ted Williams, thought that the pitchers were useless. After all, they only played every fifth day — often not even for a full game! In addition, Williams observed, pitchers can't even hit! Richie Ashburn, Hall of Fame outfielder from the Philadelphia Phillies, warned his teenage daughter that he didn't care who she brought home, as long as he wasn't a pitcher. Many pitchers equally hate the hitters. They are the enemy!

The head of the teacher's union sees the world one way — through teacher's eyes. When promoted to school principal, she becomes more and more aware of the parent pressure groups, and especially the taxpayers in the community. And then, if she is elected

Superintendent of Schools, her perceptual world changes dramatically again! She now becomes extremely aware of the school board members whose votes make or break her. As her demands shift, her responsibilities change, and she experiences a whole new world.

When you think about this perceptual myopia? It is natural? Since I spend eight hours a day, five days a week, fifty weeks a year, doing what I do, my awareness of the company is 90% from my view. Plus, the people I associate with on the job often do what I do, further reinforcing my own vantage point. And then, when I go home at night and vent to my husband, wife and friends, they become inundated with my view. They acquire my perspective, they understand me, and even play back my viewpoint to me constantly. Because they care, they provide further support for my "neighborhood" view of the universe of our company!

Respecting involves empathizing and taking the time to understand the perspective of others with different responsibilities. and then communicating my appreciation of their high and low experiences with the resultant feelings they may have about their work.

Take some time to imagine and experience the daily grind of community members from departments other than your own.

. . . .

🔆 TURNING IT ON

Sharing Roles Together

Take a few minutes to walk a mile in the roles of others whose work is different from yours. See how well you understand the unique pressures, stresses, challenges, joys and rewards in their work.

After expressing your thoughts about their daily work, ask your teammates to add any other details you may have so that you can get a fuller picture.

_____

_____

_____

_____

_____

_____

_____

_____

_____

_____

. . . .

. . . .

 TURNING IT ON

Getting by with a Little Help
from Your Friends

Now, ask those with different responsibilities than your own to communicate their understanding of your own unique pressures, stresses, challenges, joys and rewards at work. Then add to their thoughts anything they may have missed, to help expand their picture of your work.

_____

_____

_____

_____

_____

_____

Hopefully, in this new expanded picture and better view, the world starts to take its truer shape and appearance to us. It would be as if the picture of the world, through the New Yorker's eyes, started taking on its truer perspective. The Pacific Ocean becomes significantly bigger than the Atlantic. Canada becomes larger than New York City. And New Zealand is included!

. . . .

CHAPTER 15

INSPIRING:

Connecting each person's contribution in changing the world (The why? of the community)

> *We thought we were racing a sailboat, but we found we were changing a nation!*
>
> *– Captain John Bertram*
> *On Australia's Winning The America's Cup*

Ultimately, why do we really do what we do? We are inspiring others and ourselves, when we are reminding our community of higher, more positive human purposes for our work.

---

1. Climb Higher and Discover the Ultimate Positive Purpose of Your Work
2. Re-frame the Ultimate Purpose of Your Work to Give Your Reason Energy and Positive Feelings

---

1. Climb Higher and Discover the Ultimate Positive Purpose of Your Work

I (Lew Lesoncy) once listened to police from Delaware describe the day-to-day pressures and stresses in their work. Sure, most of us are aware of some of these challenges, but my eyes were opened to many others that I hadn't considered. Imagine, going for a day or two, experiencing few major incidents, and than in an instant being confronted with a life and death challenge. You could always be just seconds away. Each morning when you leave home and say "so long" to your loved ones, you never know if this is "the day."

During our forty-five hours together, I was struck with the great professionalism each one of the members of the force exhibited. Towards the end of the graduate school course, some other subtleties emerged in the classroom. Due to the huge challenges the police officers face, spending a disproportionate amount of time working with people who are breaking the law, one officer confided that he occasionally experienced a cynical view of human nature. His work was so focused on the negative. This, of course, was quite understandable, considering he was constantly racing up and down US Route 1, writing tickets for people who are upset and blaming the world. There wasn't time to stop the compliant driver and hand her a certificate for, let's say, a Grotto pizza, for driving at the posted speed limit!

We encouraged the group to begin thinking about the positive nature of their work. Why do they do what they are doing? What "positive" gifts do these defenders of the law ultimately bring to their community? After getting beyond removing the criminal from the street or punishing the lawbreaker, we discovered a higher purpose.

"Well, we provide 'security' for our citizens, don't we?" — a young trooper volunteered. The mood in the room lightened when a sergeant added, "We are defenders of justice making sure every one is 'treated equally' according to the law." A third suggested, "You could say we are a source of 'reassurance' for our communities."

"Speaking of reassurance, wouldn't you say 'caring' is an important part of what we do?" the elder in the room suggested.

"I mean, how many flat tires have you changed for an elderly man or woman, in the dark middle of the night. I'd call that caring and reassurance."

After a full hour of exploring the higher purpose (the why?) of their work, it was obvious that the course ended on an upbeat note. The class's energy level was elevated, and it appeared many left the course with a more inspiring view of their important work. Their work transcended simply dealing with individual lawbreakers, and resulted in them finding that they were at the very heart of providing security for the people of the First State!

Even in work that, at first glance, has negative tasks associated with it, you can ultimately find a more "positive" view of the same challenges.

Jim, thanks to your efforts, infection rates are way down.

2. Re-frame the Ultimate Purpose of Your Work to Give Your Reason Energy and Positive Feelings

Our friend, Carl Hausman, the piano player for the popular Kit-Kats traveled the world thrilling huge crowds, but he had a different ultimate purpose. The cheerful keyboard man simply wanted to have a little ice cream store, and to play the piano there for the neighborhood families. He gave up the big time and opened up his marble countered, old wooden floor shop in Sinking Spring, Pennsylvania, making his own ice cream while displaying glass jars of candy on top of the ice cream cabinets. On weekends, families gathered, ate their sundaes, drank their milk shakes and listened to Carl playing ragtime.

When asked if he likes selling ice cream, Carl smiles and explains, "You never see an unhappy person in an ice cream shop. Whether they buy anything or not, they are happy. You might say that what we are selling is not ice cream. We are selling happiness!"

Speaking of how Carl Hausman views his higher purpose of playing the piano, singer-songwriter Billy Joel describes the nature of his work in the "Piano Man" as helping people "relax," because "Its me they've been coming to see to forget about life for a while."

All of Carl's team members knew what their ultimate product really was . . . happiness! Carl re-framed what he was actually selling to connect its impact on to peoples' lives. He also created energy and positive feelings for his work life.

Perhaps the brightest place to be in the quaint little town of Great Barrington, Massachusetts is Robin's Candy Store. Snugly nestled in the heart of the Berkshire Mountains, Robin's welcoming windows invite you in like a crackling fireplace does on a snowy day. You feel warm, alive and young again, basking in visual, tactile, gustatory delights while being moved by the lifting music in the background. You want to play again, while tasting the best licorice you ever had in your life. Robin's thousands of candies, in their spotless glass jars, make you feel like you are still staring up at them like you did as a child. You never want to leave Robin's. Like a sweet amusement park, Robin wanted to create great feelings of being away in fantasyland — right there on Main Street in Great Barrington, Massachusetts.

. . . .

💡 TURNING IT ON

Inspiring Yourself as a World Changer

How does your work make the world a better place?

_____

_____

_____

_____

_____

_____

_____

_____

_____

_____

. . . .

. . . .

☀ TURNING IT ON

Realizing Your Impact on People

How many lives does your work directly or indirectly touch?

In what ways? Imagine a typical benefit you offer to people.

_____

_____

_____

_____

_____

_____

_____

_____

_____

_____

. . . .

CHAPTER 16

CELEBRATING:

Recognizing efforts, improvements and progress

What the caterpillar calls the end of the world, the master calls a butterfly.

– Richard Bach

Success is important, but proceeding from only a success-failure mentality is not only linear; it is limiting.

As our company became the leader in its field, driven by its ultimate "why" of helping the people we serve become successful, some within the organization starting taking their eyes off our ultimate purpose. As the leader in our industry, some became obsessed with being the leader, while others kept the focus on our original inspirational purpose. What resulted from the "being #1 thinking," was curious. Allow us an analogy at this point to explain the limiting effects of the "You either win or you lose mentality."

Imagine that you are a jockey in a horserace — and you're riding the fastest horse. As you ride, are you looking forward to the finish line, or at looking back at how far your competitors are behind? If you turn around and notice the closest competitor is actually far away, do you relax a little because you are going to achieve your limited goal of winning? Or do you keep your eye on the finish line, run the best possible race of your life, and go forward?

The question to ask is: "Should our reason for being — our purpose — be compromised because our competitor has lost its motivation?" Isn't a better standard — rather than success vs. failure: One that reflects our current :self vs. our best self?" If so, than our focus shifts from asking each other not, "Did you win or did you lose?" — but rather, "How are you growing?" and "What did you learn on your road to becoming your best?" In these moments we are using the relating process of celebrating, or we are centering on efforts, improvements and progress.

> 1. Celebrating Involves Sensitivity to a Person's Efforts
> 2. Celebrating Involves Sensitivity to Improvements and Progress

1. Celebrating Involves Sensitivity to a Person's Efforts

The little one puts on her shoes for the very first time — the first time ever in her life. She is so proud, as she walks over to mom and dad to share this monumental achievement. She is awaiting the applause for her accomplishment.

"Mommy, daddy, look. I put on my
shoes all by myself!"

She looks up.

Mommy looks down and responds,

"They're on the wrong feet!"

In a small way, the little one is learning — don't do anything unless you can do it perfectly. Only perfect (success) is valued.

In the inspiring company, the culture is a dramatically different because the effort itself has value (After all, how can people do more than they can do?)

Imagine a more celebrating approach.

"Mommy, daddy, look. I put my shoes on all by myself!"

"You must be proud of yourself honey. This is a big day for you. Yesterday, you couldn't do this and you tried and put them on all by yourself. Congratulations!"

"How do they feel?

"Well, they don't feel as good as when you put them on Mommy."

"Maybe you can find even a better way to put your shoes on this important day. Let's think about what you can try next."

"Hmm, the other one on the other one?"

"Try it."

Struggling.

"They feel better. I put my shoes on all by myself!"

How many times does someone hesitate offering a new idea because he or she isn't sure if everyone else will like it? When we live in a culture that values everyone looking for better ways, we aren't afraid of taking risks that offer us new routes to reach our driving purpose (the why?).

. . . .

💡 TURNING IT ON

Catching Efforts

You are catching an effort, when you are noticing someone offering a new idea, or a better way. When you think about it, in those moments the person is taking a risk. Recall your teammates — the ones who were willing to try something new. Who on your team has made efforts this year, or in the past, that you noticed? Make sure you share that you caught (noticed) the person's effort with them. And, yes, watch the person's face as you share that you noticed, because you will be in touch with them at a higher level. You noticed the risk they took!

. . . .

2.   Celebrating Involves Sensitivity to Improvements and Progress

When celebrating, we are listening with sensitive antennae to any growth, movement or form or progress our teammates are experiencing. Going from no sales to one sale is immeasurable statistically. And moving from one sale to two truly, doubles sales! Just as importantly, "comforting" points out progress. Yesterday I was here. Today I am here. Where could I be tomorrow?

After being rejected by a potential big customer, the young sales person had a decision to make. In her next meeting, she bounces her dilemma off her inspiring sales manager.

"Should I go back or just forget about it?"

The upbeat leader responds with animation,

> *"Actually, Brenda you have nothing to lose if you go back because they are not currently your account. This is an easy decision the more you think of it. Perhaps you can develop a plan to get them excited about what our product can mean to them if we become their distributor in the long run."*

After listening to her sales manager, Brenda was determined to develop her presentation and a plan tailored to the needs of this particular business. As her inspiring sales manager listens to Brenda's new presentation, she comforts by zeroing in on the progress Brenda made and reveals a few small additional tips to excite the customer. Brenda is buoyed up by her inspiring leader, to believe that she can do it.

And, by the way, the manager knew exactly the time of the meeting and called her sales person an hour later. Instead of starting her conversation off with the standard, "Did they buy?" (success-failure mentality) she comforts by enthusiastically revealing, "You are really progressing — look at how far you have brought yourself. How are you feeling?"

Men, this is our quarter!

That's something you would only hear in the turned ON community. The long-term goal is to lift the spirits during both the highs and lows of life.

. . . .

💡 TURNING IT ON

Catching Improvements and Progress

Think of all of the people who have improved and progressed since you have been with your company? Do a "before-and-after" on these people.

Reflect on where they were "before" in their skills, their attitude and their performance. Now reflect on where they are today. Most importantly, share with the person your before-and-after picture of him or her. Watch the turn ON power of comforting- you caught them growing!

. . . .

PART IV

RECHARGE

Our Backup, Renewable Energy Source, In Case of Power Failure

"Recharging" is another way of turning our feelings ON in regard to our experiences at work. Recharging offers us our own personal light and can be used at any time when the power system in our outside environment is down.

When the sockets in the four walls and ceiling aren't working and when the light switches are failing us, recharging offers us immediate light.

The advantage of using this personal backup system inside us, is that we need nothing else, and no one else, to provide any inspirational light. We have our own facility to keep our workspace lit. Recharging offers us a time to reflect on our work in new ways to give us insights to keep us turned ON and going forward.

RECHARGE BY REFLECTING ON THE PERSONAL MEANING OF YOUR WORK

If we do not plant knowledge when young, it will give us no shade when we are old.

– Lord Chesterfield

Personal Growth

How have you grown since you have been working for your company?

Pride

Of what accomplishment are you most proud?

Self-Esteem

How has your work changed your belief in yourself?

Creativity

Which of your own ideas has your company used?

Security

What security have you earned through your work?

Love

What do you most love about your work?

Courage

What were some moments of courage for you at work?

Curiosity

How can you use your curiosity to grow even further on your job?

Overcoming a Challenge

What challenges have you had in the past and overcame?

Challenge

What is your biggest challenge today? How can you give positive meaning to give you the motivation to overcome it?

RECHARGE BY REFLECTING ON THE SKILLS YOU HAVE ACQUIRED

> *A man who finds no satisfaction in himself will seek for it in vain elsewhere.*
>
> *– François de La Rochefoucauld*

Skill-Refinement

What technical skills have you developed since being with your company?

Task Mastery Over Specific Skills

What have you mastered and do really well?
What are you best at?

Task Progress

In what area of your work are you really progressing?

Correction

Describe a mistake you made and corrected.

Problem Solving

What problems did your team have at work that you helped solve?

Future Improvement

What task or skill are you going to work on this year?

RECHARGE BY REFLECTING ON THE PEOPLE CONNECTIONS YOU MADE THROUGH YOUR WORK

Don't worry when you are not recognized, but strive to be worthy of recognition."

— Abraham Lincoln

Rewarding Relationships

What rewarding relationships have you found in your work community?

Support

Who offers you support when you are down and out?

Belonging

With which group do you feel you belong?

Contributing

To whom have you contributed to help make
become better?

Encouraging

Who do you believe in, saw their potential, and told them?

RECHARGE BY REFLECTING ON THE PROGRESS YOUR TEAM MADE

> *Wisdom alone is true ambition's aim, wisdom is the source of virtue and of fame; obtained with labour, for mankind employed, and then, when most you share it, best enjoyed.*
>
> *— Alfred North Whitehead*

Mutual Respect

Who on your team do you respect and sense respects you?

Mutual Progress

With whom on your team do you especially feel you are growing?

Synergy of Ideas

With whom on your team do you brainstorm new ideas to make things happen?

Team Theming

What makes your team special?
How is your team unique?

Winning Team

What are some of the things you have accomplished together?

Open Communications

With whom can you communicate both the good and bad news about your work? Who can you be extremely honest with for the purpose of making things better?

RECHARGE BY REFLECTING ON THE IMPACT YOU HAD ON YOUR CUSTOMERS

> *For us, our most important stakeholder is not our stockholders, it is our customers.*
>
> *– John Mackey*

Touching Lives

How many of your customers are directly and indirectly touched by your work?

Connecting to My Customer

How does your specific job add value to your customer's life?

Customer Sensitivity

As you walk a mile in your customer's shoes, what are you most sensitive to about your customer's needs?

Striving For Perfection in Customer Service

What are some examples where you insisted on using better ways to serve your customers?

Customer Humanizing

Where have you consciously treated a customer as a unique, special important human being?

RECHARGE BY REFLECTING ON THE POSITIVE WAYS YOUR WORK AFFECTS YOUR FAMILY AND COMPANY

> *Probably no greater honor can come to any man than the respect of his colleagues.*
>
> *– Cary Grant*

Fulfilling Dream

How are you helping your community reach your dreams together?

Living Community Values

Where was an example of a choice you made to live by your values?

Feeling Empowered

When has your company trusted
you to make a decision?

Family Benefits

How has your work improved your family?

RECHARGE BY REFLECTING ON THE INFLUENCE YOUR WORK HAS ON YOUR SPIRITUAL GROWTH

> *Doing good to others is not a duty, it is a joy,*
> *for it increases our own health and happiness.*
>
> *– Zoroaster*

Self-Actualizing at Work

Where in your work are you growing toward becoming the best person you are capable of being?

Spirit

What gives you the most satisfaction in your work? What evokes your spirit?

Passion

What do you believe in more than anything else about your work?

Flow

When are you most yourself in your work, totally immersed in the work itself?

Transcendence

Re-experience the most fulfilling moment of your work life?

Visualizing

Envision an ideal great future achievement for you at work.

God at Work

How are you connecting your work to your spiritual life?

ON

It is our heartfelt hope that, in a small way, you have taken a second look at your daily work and how it contributes towards making the world a little bit better.

You also improve the world by lifting the spirits of those around you, helping them realize that their efforts are making a difference. By changing our individual view of our work, by finding a higher vantage point, we can see so much more, and so much more clearly.

We also have another hope -- an important one. We would be thrilled if you agreed that ideas such as comforting, inspiring, loving, encouraging, electrifying, and respecting can be brought into your own personal life, to inspire your loved ones. You can change the world in many ways, each time you offer a kind word and some hope.

If the world is going to have more purpose and spirit, it has to start somewhere with someone who chooses to bring more joy and meaning to others. It can be you. And remember, just because you can't do everything doesn't mean you can't do anything. And isn't doing some-thing better than doing no-thing?

Keep the Light ON.

Inspirationally,

Lewis Losoncy

Colin Walsh

ACKNOWLEDEMENTS

Lewis Losoncy

Thanks to Gabi Losoncy for your excellent research work, initial editing and quote finding. Thanks Diane Losoncy for always being there in many ways, sensing what was important on a moment-to-moment basis, adding insightful thoughts from the vantage point of both a wife and a psychologist.

This book was written from the model of the inspiring and passionate members of the Matrix family. You thought your products were shampoos and colors, and you found that you were building the pride and prosperity of hundreds of thousands of salon professionals. We proved together that corporate doesn't automatically mean cold, and that a job doesn't have to mean work. And, thanks to Caroline Walsh for taking the time to put a new light in *ON*. You also helped us get rid of every weak "nook and Kenny!"

Thanks Colin Walsh. Your refreshing presence breathed new life, energy and power into what will eventually be hundred of thousands of people. *ON* is now becoming the new way-of-being in the hallways from 5th Avenue to Main Street America. Your leadership proves that spirit and purpose can grow passionate people anywhere, even in the corporate world. Thank you for giving me the opportunity to help our family turn the lights *ON*, to our dream together again.

Colin Walsh

A special thank you to Caroline Walsh for your unyielding love, support and advice in making *ON* a reality. My heartfelt appreciation goes out to Ronald and Jillian Walsh, for defining what it meant to be ON through your every word and action. Thanks to the most remarkable people I could ever hope to share a dream with, including Pat Parenty, Elisa Fischer, Kathy Cullin, Martin Dale, and Naika D'Haiti. You move me to a higher place each and every day. Last, but certainly not least, to my truly inspirational friend, Lew Losoncy. You are the driving force behind our book and a recurring source of my undying gratitude.

Lewis Losoncy and Colin Walsh

Thanks to our publisher at DC Press, Dennis McClellan. Nothing is ever a problem for you. At least you never took us through it, if it was. Every author in the world ought to be lucky enough to have one book published by DC Press. They would quickly sense your point of difference there. To Carolyn Lea, thanks for always being there to clean and shine words up. To Deb Deysher, for your layout and internal design...thanks. To Greg Schultz, your cover is outstanding. And to Smoke Bechtold, your illustrations are simply outstanding.

ABOUT THE AUTHORS

Dr. Lewis Losoncy is a respected motivational psychologist, speaker and author of 25 books on topics ranging from encouragement, positive attitude, success, leadership, and teamwork. Known as "The Doctor of Encouragement," he has taken his ideas on building motivated people through the creation of inspirational culture to audiences in all 50 U.S. states, all Canadian provinces, Australia, Mexico, Thailand, and a dozen European countries. He has been an encouraging influence on companies from Matrix (a division of L'Oreal) to S.C. Johnson, Hermann-Miller to Boeing, Dell,, as well as educators, psychologists, social workers, and government agencies. "Dr. Lew," as his many followers call him, has appeared on CNN and CBS This Morning, and has written for and appeared on the pages of Psychology Today, The Wall Street Journal, Science of the Mind, Working Woman, and Prevention. Lew lives with his wife Diane and daughter Gabrielle in Melbourne, FL and Philadelphia, PA.

. . . .

Colin Walsh is the Vice President and General Manager of Matrix USA, a division of L'Oreal. Colin has been described as an industry "game changer" and his leadership style has earned him respect and the reputation of a "renegade." As a passionate speaker on the topic of inspiration and leadership, Colin shares his perspective on working with a purpose, here in ON. He resides in New York City with his wife Caroline and son Jonah and daughter Sienna.

CONTACT THE AUTHORS

You are encouraged to contact the authors with your questions, comments, suggestions, and thoughts regarding the concept of "ON."

The authors are available for speaking, keynoting, and workshops. Should you have an interest in having one or both of the authors participate in an event your organization or company is planning in the future, please contact us at:

info@dcpressbooks.com
Subject Line: "ON" – Authors

Telephone: 407-417-1855

Please tell us the following, when making contact about an event:

- Date(s) of Event
- Name of Organization/Company and State
- # of Participants Anticipated
- Topic to be addressed (keynote, workshop)
- Anticipated length of speech/address
- Contact Person and Telephone and Email Information

PRESS LLC

SANFORD • FLORIDA

Index